T0165861

Why
Unanswered
Questions,
Not
Unquestioned
Answers,
Build Faith

The Value of
DOUB†

BILL TAMMEUS

Walking Together, Finding the Way ®
SKYLIGHT PATHS®
PUBLISHING
Nashville, Tennessee

Skylight Paths Publishing
an imprint of Turner Publishing Company
Nashville, Tennessee
New York, New York

www.skylightpaths.com
www.turnerpublishing.com

The Value of Doubt:
Why Unanswered Questions, Not Unquestioned Answers, Build Faith

2016 Quality Paperback Edition, First Printing
© 2016 by William D. Tammeus

Library of Congress Cataloging-in-Publication Data
Names: Tammeus, Bill, author.
Title: The value of doubt : why unanswered questions, not unquestioned
  answers, build faith / Bill Tammeus.
Description: Woodstock, VT : SkyLight Paths Publishing, 2016. | Includes
  bibliographical references.
Identifiers: LCCN 2016024609| ISBN 9781594736315 (pbk.) | ISBN 9781594736391
  (ebook)
Subjects: LCSH: Faith.
Classification: LCC BV4637 .T36 2016 | DDC 234/.23—dc23 LC record available at
https://lccn.loc.gov/2016024609

10 9 8 7 6 5 4 3 2 1

Manufactured in the United States of America
Cover Design: Jenny Buono
Cover Art: Ollyy / shutterstock.com
Interior Design: Jenny Buono

This book is dedicated

to the grandchildren

whom my wife, Marcia, and I share:

Olivia and Jacob; Cole and Piper;

Lucy and Zoe; and Ava and Scarlett.

May they cherish their inevitable journeys through the valley of

doubt and may they discover the light of faith.

Contents

Introduction

·⌇·

We live by metaphor, by myth, by allegory. There is no other way.

I learned this when I was eleven years old. It was Easter Sunday 1956 and I was attending a sunrise service outside of Kellogg Church near Woodstock School in Landour-Mussoorie, India, with other Woodstock students.

In the foothills of the Himalayas that day, the air was sharp but welcoming, supplely fragile but not brittle. At the eastern edge of the horizon two hills formed a V, and we observed the sun rising in the very center of that V, prodigally exploding light and hope into the expectant, dark air.

I came to believe in resurrection that morning, though I probably did not have the vocabulary to begin to articulate what that meant. And I'm sure all these years later that there is no vocabulary adequate to that task. I also began to discern then—as much as an eleven-year-old could—that metaphor, myth, and allegory are the foundations on which we build the castles of our reality.

What does that mean? Well, I just told you that the sun rose that sweet Easter daybreak. It did not. The sun never rises in the way that those words suggest. What happens, of course, is that the earth spins on its axis and the spot on which I happen to be located in the morning inches into the sunlight. In the same way, in the evening the sun does not set. The earth, instead, twirls away from its light. (Though, of course, both bodies are in motion, meaning that although Galileo was mostly right in his argument with the Catholic Church, the church—sort of like a stopped watch that's correct twice a day—was also a little bit right.)

We all know that about our sunrise/sunset language but we continue to use those words, nonetheless. Metaphor, myth, allegory.

And if we describe the events, conditions, and circumstances of our daily lives in those ways, how much more are metaphor, myth, and allegory at the root of religious faith? As I say, we have no choice about relying on metaphor if we are to use words at all, for all words—even those in sacred writ—are metaphors, pointing beyond themselves to some condition, thing, person, or action. Our only other choice is silence, and sometimes silence—despite its many benefits—says too much, leaves open too many options, fails to draw necessary boundaries. Psalm 119:105 describes God's word as a "lamp before my feet, and a light for my journey" (CEB).[1] Silence, by contrast, sometimes can mean no light at all.

> All words—even those in sacred writ—are metaphors, pointing beyond themselves.

Not long ago I had a conversation with a young Kenyan woman who has been in the United States for five years but whose heart still aches because of Africa's many wounds. She is Christian and wishes to love and respect people of other faith traditions because, as she told me, "Nobody knows who is right."

When she said that, I looked at her with relief and satisfaction. "That," I told her, "is the beginning of wisdom." That it also may be the beginning of heresy is part of the problem of the human condition.

I have spent part of my career in journalism writing about faith, and most of my life trying to live out faith, a word and a predisposition that has a million definitions. Perhaps the most famous comes from Hebrews 11:1: "Now faith is the substance of things hoped for, the evidence of things not seen" (KJV). Although it's famous, I've never thought of that Hebrews definition as especially helpful, except as an example of why the world of faith is filled with paradox, with indirection, with a sense that however we articulate our faith at any given moment it's always provisional and will need to be reformulated at some point. My contention born out of experience is that one of the best ways—perhaps the only way—to reformulate faith is by exploring our doubts about it. Authentic, living, vibrant faith also must come with a foundational lack of literalness that should drive biblical literalists crazy, though it doesn't seem to, given that they often simply ignore all that.

So in this book I will try to give you some ideas about what faith and doubt might be, what they have meant to me, and what they might mean to you. I also will challenge you to rethink it all for yourself. It's time I do that. As I write this, it's pushing toward sixty years since that Easter morning in India, where my family lived for two years when my father was part of a University of Illinois agriculture team assigned to help with what came to be called the Green Revolution. (Nice work, Dad.)

If I wait another 60 years, I'll be more than 130 years old—and I have no faith that my memory would be as clear then.

APPROACHING DOUBT

Is faith a list of rules?

On wintry Sunday mornings, Grandpa Helander would leave the house at 901 East Twelfth Street in Streator, Illinois—about a hundred miles south of where we lived in Woodstock, Illinois—and go to the nearby detached garage so he could start and then warm up the 1948 ivory Chrysler for Grandma. He wanted her to be comfortable on the way to church.

I saw this over and over again when we would visit them on their edge-of-town farm, where my mother grew up. Grandpa would wear a suit—sometimes with a vest—and tie, along with a topcoat and hat. Grandma wore one of her better dresses, a warm coat, and inevitably some kind of hat, too.

When they got to Park Presbyterian Church, where, by the way, I was baptized on Easter Sunday 1945, they found their usual seats on the right side of the sanctuary, greeting friends as they moved in. And there they were nearly every Sunday—Swedes who had come to this country about the turn of the century as Lutherans and who became Presbyterian because, well, I'm not sure why. It's one of the thousands of questions I now wish I had asked them.

My maternal grandparents did not speak much about religious faith. Faith was not so much a list of rules and doctrines as it was something simply to be lived. When I thought about this later, I decided that for them faith meant these things: They believed that some kind of god existed, and they would have said it was the God in whom Christians believe; they were committed to their congregation; they said grace before meals; they were charitable in countless ways; they loved each other and their two daughters. Grandma was strong, but sweet and hospitable to a fault. Grandpa worked hard, loved a good joke as much

3

as he loved his King Edward cigars, and had sometimes-inflexible opinions, including the idea that Slavs weren't good people. I don't think his church taught him that latter notion, although over the centuries the church has taught its adherents some dreadful ideas.

From what I could tell as a boy and later as a young man, faith to my maternal grandparents meant being dependable, consistent, self-reliant—all the while recognizing that something was at play in the universe that could not be explained, something or someone who might even care for the people who wondered about that something or someone. They were happy to label that something "God" and to locate themselves within the theological boundaries of mainline Protestantism. To mean much of anything, religion requires some kind of choice, some kind of commitment. Just as you can't simply speak "language" but must pick one, so it is with religion. Otherwise it's just what they say politics ain't—beanbag.

> Just as you can't simply speak "language" but must pick one, so it is with religion.

In the Helander household, however, there was not a lot of room for exploring religious ideas. Doubt was not an especially welcome guest, though my grandparents were not fundamentalists of any stripe.

One day as we still sat at the dining room table after our post-church Sunday fried chicken dinner, the adults began talking about, well, something religious, I guess. Like most kids in such situations, I wasn't paying much attention. Until, that is, I heard my father say this: "Well, for all I know Buddha was the son of God, too."

For just an awkward second the room was silent. I couldn't wait to see who would take his bait. I was not surprised that my mother, after catching her stunned breath, replied, "Oh, Bill ..." (he went by that name, too), in a deeply drawn-out, dismissive tone of voice. She aimed a tactical verbal nuke at Dad's idea, bull's-eyed the target, and obliterated it. He never brought it up again then or later, at least within earshot of me.

And yet something in me was proud of Dad for the comment. Something in me opened up to the possibility that odd and even heretical religious ideas might at least be worth talking about. He gave me space for doubt. But the closest my parents ever came to confronting such ideas was to acknowledge their existence, especially in the context of India, where we met Muslims and Hindus, Sikhs and Jains, along with a variety of Christians and the occasional Buddhist (although Buddha was from the Indian subcontinent, Buddhists aren't numerous in India). We children understood that we were to treat such people with respect, but somehow that respect, as it emanated from our parents (or at least from Mom), seemed tinged with a bit of pity that, unlike us, others did not

> Odd and even heretical religious ideas might at least be worth talking about.

have the truth. Though, of course, in the words of the old spiritual, all of us were standing in the need of prayer.

The hint of false certitude in which our religious thought at the time could be found in our family was troubling to me. But I was just a kid with a kid's agenda, meaning I didn't think about that very much. It would be several more years before I would begin to entertain irregular religious ideas and even embrace some on my way to something like Christian orthodoxy, lowercase o.

For the time being, I was happy with this occasional thought: "Buddha? Where'd that come from, Dad?"

LET'S TALK ABOUT THIS

What early memories do you have of learning about faith and how much of what you picked up then still guides you?

Did your family of origin encourage free-ranging discussion about religion or were you simply given answers you were expected to accept?

Does faith require maximum clarity?

I no longer have the physical evidence for what I'm about to write, but I believe that the Reverend Wes Stevens, pastor of the Congregational Unitarian-Universalist Church (or CongoUniUni, as it was known) in Woodstock, offered a closing prayer at my eighth-grade graduation ceremony in 1959 at Clarence Olson Junior High School.

Whether it was there or somewhere else, the important thing for me was something he said: "Help us remember that divine possibilities are always possibilities."

Although I have slipped that line into a cranial shoebox that I've stashed on a back shelf and not dragged out for a long time, over the years it has come back to me again and again as a welcome, encouraging visitor from another time, ready to nudge me back to faith, back to living with a sense of the imaginable in the midst of the unimaginable.

I'll have more to say about the Holy Trinity later, but as a Trinitarian I am obliged to try to conceive of how the Father, the Son, and the Holy Spirit, as the traditional formulation goes, might be different persons while also being the same God, who is one. This theological system of mystical enumeration has confounded people of faith since the first time a follower of Jesus drew the Trinitarian implication out of a careful, openhearted reading of scripture, which never uses the term "Trinity."[1] People have come up with many ways to explain the Trinity: It's like an apple, with skin, the fruit, and seeds. Or it's like water, which can be ice, liquid, or steam, a gas. Many of these explanations simply introduce ideas eventually declared heretical. And yet within its complex web of meanings the Trinity contains a picture of a divine community of love in which each of the three persons is in perfect and loving harmony and relationship with each of the others. Nothing the Father does or thinks is ever in conflict with anything the Son or the Spirit does or thinks and nothing the Son does or thinks ... well, you get the idea.

Over the years, I have come to draw on Wes Stevens's phrasing to conclude that the Holy Spirit is, for me, the God of possibilities—especially when it seems that I have run out of possibilities. Which is to say that the Spirit is the one who can create options, openings, and opportunities where and when none seems to exist. If insanity is doing the same thing again and again while expecting a different result, faith is doing the same thing again and again while being open to some (by definition, surprising) result that we simply are unable to think of on our own. Perhaps that equates faith with insanity, and I know some atheists, particularly those among the more aggressive so-called New Atheists, who would say that, indeed, faith is insane. But it is precisely that engagement of God's wisdom and humanity's foolishness[2] that makes faith so attractive to some people, including me, for, even in the face of our doubts, it leads us to trust in spite of what can seem like convincing evidence to the contrary.

> The Spirit is the one who can create options, openings, and opportunities where and when none seem to exist.

One recent Christmas, the annual holiday letter from my friend W. Paul Jones, a Trappist monk and Catholic priest, arrived with this forlorn conclusion based on his (and others') repeated failure to get the state of Missouri to abolish the death penalty: "How absurdly I live, insisting that totally unwilling legislators render 'humane' a system for which abolition is the only moral option." But, simultaneously, he could write this:

> Yet hope perseveres as a *bas relief* in the form of a "remnant"—those reborn of a refining fire, persistently faithful, hidden with Christ in God, defiantly living the love that enables loving—serving as "stars shining in

the midst of a depraved generation." Imprisoned physi-
cally in the heart of a rival empire, St. Paul challenges
us, the fledgling church, never "to grow tired of doing
good; for if we continue to struggle on, we shall reap
our harvest in due season." Faith, says Jesus and sings
Mendelssohn, is the gift of "enduring to the end." ...
Advent is the gift-wrapped capacity to defy a society
turned backwards, hope in the face of a sneering cyni-
cism, and wager on whispered guesses blowing in the
wind with hints of being Holy.

When, after nearly twenty-seven years, my first marriage ended and my
wife soon after married our former pastor, the man with whom she had
been having an affair while he still was our pastor, I thought that not
just my marital present but also any marital future was done, foreclosed,
empty. And, in many ways, I was fine with that. I had come into that
marriage as a whole (if immature) human being, and despite the mis-
takes both of us had made, I had left it whole (and immature in different
ways). And I was expecting—and willing—to spend the rest of my life
single, being a father to my two adult daughters and a grandfather to
any children they might someday have.

But within a few months of my divorce becoming final, a marvelous
woman with the same first name as my first wife walked into my life
and opened up unimagined possibilities
for relationship, for family, for a future
remarkably different from the rather
lonesome one I had been willing to settle
for. The next year, both at age fifty-one,
we married, and we blended our six chil-
dren (all but two of whom were out on their own by then) into what
has become truly a family.

> Faith doesn't require
> astonishing and
> instantaneous insights.

It is hard for me to attribute this gift of grace to God or spe-
cifically to the God of possibilities, the Holy Spirit. I simply don't
know. But I am willing to conceive of that possibility. And who could
disprove it?

One of my former associate pastors, Ron Roberts, used to say that he can't really detect the hand of God moving in his life while he's in the midst of living it. It's only later when he looks back that he sees how there may well have been a divine plan that played out just the way it would have played out had there been, in fact, a divine plan. I'm with Ron on that. My God radar isn't very good in the hot moment. And, frankly, later I'm still speculating, even if with a bit more clarity.

But faith doesn't require maximum clarity, astonishing and instantaneous insights into what Father Paul Jones called "whispered guesses blowing in the wind with hints of being Holy." Such clarity, such insights might well blind us to the truth that divine possibilities are always possibilities. And that would be a high price to pay as we lose track of the reality that the questions faith and doubt raise are at least as important as the answers toward which they point us.

LET'S TALK ABOUT THIS

Some of the so-called New Atheists say having faith in God is insane. What, if any, part of faith strikes you as insane?

How close to what I call "maximum clarity" do you need to get to be comfortable with your faith?

Describe your level of comfort when it comes to ambiguity and paradox in other parts of your life not directly related to religion.

Why is idolatry so damn attractive?

In the collection of slides that my parents took when we lived in India, there's one of two children standing in front of a small roadside temple, inside of which are idols of some sort.

In the photo, the inside of the temple is too dark to see just what kind of idols dwell there, but in Hinduism—in the end, a monotheistic faith (oh, it is too)—the Upanishads say there may be 330 million gods, so the choice of which one to place in a roadside temple is pretty much wide open. One explanation sometimes given for that huge number of gods is that it represents the approximate population of the world when the Upanishads were written, thus metaphorically meaning that each person believed in his or her own god, just as some religion scholars today say that Americans believe in some 300 million different gods.

Our ability to describe God is so pathetically limited that all such efforts are doomed. And as poet Christian Wiman writes in *My Bright Abyss: Meditation of a Modern Believer*, "The minute you speak with certitude about God, he is gone."[3] Still, we continue to try out descriptions. Somehow to put flesh on the spiritual bones of God seems like a task that we simply must undertake. Something in us drives us toward what becomes anthropomorphism. For Christians, this task is made infinitely easier, though still not a snap, because we assert that God already has put flesh on God's own spiritual bones in the form of Jesus of Nazareth. So if we want to know what God is like we just have to look to Jesus. I like that answer but it strikes me as too simplistic, too facile, too rote, too literal, too, well, orthodox. And if that's our only answer, we're in danger of becoming unitarians of the second person of the Trinity.

The novelist Kurt Vonnegut once wrote that people go to church just "to daydream about God."[4] It's a high calling, even if Vonnegut was making light of it. To daydream about God is to remind ourselves that we are creatures, not the creator; that we are finite, not infinite; that we are improbable collections of atoms and history, and that God is, well, something else. The radical otherness of God should silence us, should encourage in us a bit of humility, though it rarely seems to. And in some sense even Christianity stands opposed to the idea of that radical otherness, in part because that idea is in at least some harmony with old Greek notions about a distant, disinterested God—the god of the deists. After all, Christianity says that all we need to know about God can be found in the man we now call Christ, who, as the wonderful hymn in Philippians 2:7–8 says, "emptied himself by taking the form of a slave and by becoming like human beings. When he found himself in the form of a human, he humbled himself by becoming obedient to the point of death, even death on a cross" (CEB).

> Our ability to describe God is so pathetically limited that all such efforts are doomed.

This self-emptying is what theologians, and worse, call "kenosis," and I suppose in some ways it is a distant cousin of the kind of self-emptying that Buddhism teaches. The difference is that Buddhists seek to clear their minds of clutter with the goal of getting rid of destructive desires, or cravings, while the kenotic Christ left behind divine prerogatives, which, while he had them, contained no imaginable destructive desires at all. (I wonder if the strange authors of the *Left Behind* series of rapture theology novels ever thought that it was Christ who, through his kenosis, in the end left behind his prerogatives on our behalf. I doubt it.)[5]

Now, of course, we are two thousand years past the incarnation and Jesus doesn't walk among us any more—save, the church would say, in spirit or in some way in the Eucharist. So the human preference for concreteness, for touchable representation, leads us to paint pictures, to make statues, to re-enflesh Christ in our midst in something like the way the idols in the roadside Hindu temple in my parents' slide are meant to embody one or more of the gods. But, dissatisfied even with all of that, we create idols—idols of wealth, power, sex, achievement, the latest whatever. You know the list of addictions as well as I do.

It should be no surprise that, ultimately, all sin comes down to idolatry. That's why the First Commandment is first: Have no other gods before me. That's really the only commandment people need, given how all the others—even the two Jesus identified as the most important ones—are wrapped up in that one. To love God and to love our neighbor, after all, are inevitable results of a commitment to having no other gods but God.

> The radical otherness of God should silence us.

Yet we are drawn to idols, feel empty without them, feel abandoned and insignificant when we don't have something that requires our worship, something easier than God to get our minds around, maybe even something the existentialist Albert Camus called "a master."

We sell ourselves easily but not cheaply to these idols. They demand of us our very souls, finally, in exchange for a simple bowl of Jacob's red stew.[6] God also invites us to commit our very selves, our souls, our spirits, our centers to God. But the exchange rate is stunningly different. When we give ourselves to God we get, via pure grace, transformation, love, the hope and promise of eternity. I do, however, often wish that the bowl of red stew didn't look so fabulous and tempting—something like, well, an idol.

LET'S TALK ABOUT THIS

What is your most seductive and destructive idol? Why?

What's the closest you've come to a description of God that is meaningful and comprehensive enough for you to live with?

Are faith and belief the same?

O ne of my former (and now late) pastors used to describe the difference between belief and faith in this simple way: Suppose we drive to the Paseo Bridge in Kansas City and just stop before crossing it to the other side of the Missouri River. Being there at one end of the bridge, we can say we believe—really, deeply believe—that the bridge will hold us and will not collapse if we try to drive or walk across it. That's belief.

By contrast, faith is getting on the bridge and crossing it. Faith, in other words, is trust in action.

It's a useful distinction that at least hints at something that makes Christianity different in emphasis from some other religious traditions. Christianity is not a set of rules by which to live. It's not a philosophical system that will help explain the mysteries of the cosmos. It's not a path to enlightenment or self-fulfillment. Well, it may contain certain elements of all those things, but as former Durham Bishop N. T. Wright argues in his book *Simply Good News*, Christianity is a response to the reality that something has happened that has changed everything.[7] That something is the resurrection of Jesus. Christians can believe it, but if they don't also trust it, they're pretty much just going to sit at the end of the bridge, afraid to move into the future.

Trust, in other words, is the proper and appropriate response to that good news. It's not an intellectual assent to the news, not an adoption of a system of spiritual exercises that will help you lead a balanced life. Instead, it's a decision to enter into what can only be considered a drastic discipleship. It is a terrible, wonderful, frightening, awesome, unnerving, satisfying experience that almost nobody does well or consistently, because it's hard, if not impossible. This allegedly meek and mild Jesus is not interested in our statements of belief, our sweet prayers, or our ability to recite the historical creeds, as much as he simply wants our hearts, our commitment in gratitude to try to live a life that will seek to demonstrate what the final reign of God will look like when it comes into full flower. It's the kind of trust displayed in the book of Daniel by Shadrach, Meshach, and Abednego. Because they were not serving or worshiping the gods of King Nebuchadnezzar, he threatened to toss them into a fiery furnace. Their response: "If our God—the one we serve—is able to rescue us from the furnace of flaming fire and from your power, Your Majesty, then let him rescue us. But if he doesn't, know this for certain, Your Majesty: we will never serve your gods or worship the gold statue you've set up" (Daniel 3:17–18 CEB). Into the fire they went, and God saved them, the story says. But that's not the point. The point is that they trusted God even if God, in their moment of direst need, didn't rescue them. That's the kind of trust I'm talking about.

> Christianity is not
> a set of rules by
> which to live.

I like the way missional church leader Michael Frost of Australia put it at a conference I attended in suburban Kansas City a few years ago: The mission of the church, he said, is not to grow the church. Rather, the mission of the church is this: "To alert the world to the universal reign of God in Christ. And we do that both by proclamation and by demonstration."[8]

And if, for example, we think that when God's reign finally comes there will be peace, we work for peace now. And if we can't bring peace to the whole world, we can work to bring peace to our own neighborhood, our own congregation, our own family, or maybe even to ourselves.

And if we think that in the kingdom of God no one will be homeless, we work to provide homes for people now to demonstrate that in the coming kingdom all will be at home in the Lord.

We don't imagine, of course, that we can bring about the final kingdom of God on Earth through our demonstration projects. That's the mistake the so-called postmillennialists make—and why they are forever disappointed. (They try to build heaven on Earth, while the premillennialists try to get us into heaven—if necessary, by something called the Rapture, which the *Left Behind* series of books exploited with such commercial success a few years ago.[9]) Even if we can't build the full reign of God here, we do believe that by our work we

> This allegedly meek and mild Jesus is not interested in our statements of belief, our sweet prayers, or our ability to recite the historical creeds, as much as he simply wants our hearts.

can draw in people who catch the vision and want to experience what Jesus himself said we could experience now, which is a taste of that full reign. It's why Jesus taught followers to pray (as the old Elizabethan language has it), "Thy kingdom come, thy will be done, on Earth as it is in heaven."

As Bishop N. T. Wright notes, when the Apostle Paul began to preach the good news, "He was not telling people about a new religious system."[10] (Indeed, Paul remained a Jew his whole life, though eventually a Jew who believed that the long-promised Jewish Messiah had come.)[11]

> Nor was he urging them to adopt a new type of morality. He wasn't offering them a new philosophy—a theory about the world, how it worked, how we could know things, how we should behave. Other teachers at the time were offering things like that, but Paul's approach was different. True, his message would eventually affect those areas, too. But many people today assume that Christianity is one or more of those things—a religion, a moral system, a philosophy. In other words, they assume that Christianity is about advice. But it wasn't and isn't. Christianity is, *simply, good news*. It is the news

that *something has happened as a result of which the world is a different place.*[12]

Faith, then, is not so much understanding God, as if that were ever possible. Instead, as Wright notes, "With God—at least, with this strange God of whom the ancient scriptures spoke—the first and most important point was not to understand him but to trust him."[13] Faith has more to do with remembering that things now are different. It's living as if they're different. It's a way of keeping an eternal perspective so that the problems of the day don't overwhelm us, because we have confidence, despite our occasional doubts, that in the end God will put all things to right, even if we can't understand how they got so screwed up in the first place and even if sometimes we blame God for the world's troubles. In a Christian context, faith is not believing ourselves into a new way of living but living ourselves into a new way of believing, knowing that we can always say, with the father who is described in Mark 9:24: "I do believe, but help me overcome my unbelief!" (NLT).

LET'S TALK ABOUT THIS

If you're a Christian, would it be easier for you if the religion simply required abiding by a set of rules? If you were God, which rules would you promulgate?

What do you imagine the reign, or kingdom, of God might look like on Earth when it comes in its fullness? Or can humans even imagine such a state?

Can you really be spiritual but not religious?

For much of the last decade or so, religious scholars and cultural observers have been keeping track of people who identify themselves as "spiritual but not religious." Indeed, there's now a shorthand way to refer to this state: SBNR.

My own experience with SBNR folks is that some of them use that terminology to explain why they're not part of a faith community and don't even want to talk about becoming part of one. They may have grown up in a church or another worshiping community but walked away for one or more reasons—some understandable, some not. Describing themselves as SBNR tends to immunize them from having to discuss in any detail the reality that they may have countless unanswered religious questions but too many other interests and commitments ever to ask them. (Really, is there a more important topic than God, even if you deny that God exists?) In addition, our American culture tends to give a wide berth to people who at least have thought enough about this matter to declare themselves SBNR. It's often what passes for intellectual engagement these days. So not many SBNRs get asked follow-up questions. The declaration that one is SBNR tends to cut off the conversation or at least move

> Really, is there a more important topic than God, even if you deny that God exists?

it in the direction of why "organized religion" (often a pejorative term in the hands of many SBNR folks) has failed.

True spirituality has to do with awe, with wonder, with an openness to the inexplicable beauty of the creation and its creatures. In some sense, it is the necessary door that eventually can open to religion, which, in turn, can offer deeper theological explanations about who has created those things, matter, and people that cause us to react with awe, wonder, and openness, and even about why the creation exists at all.

Eventually, I've decided, spirituality should give birth to religion in the sense that without religion there is no serious, thoughtful, careful way to draw conclusions about what produces spirituality. Which means that spirituality is the gateway to religion, the opening of the religious question. But if it stops there, it keeps people who need to check into a hotel stuck in the lobby.

Religion, in turn, fails if it then abandons or minimizes awe, wonder, and an openness to the mysteries of beauty. Part of the task of religion is, instead, to help create categories into which we can put our conclusions about initial causes and origins and ongoing maintenance of whatever moves us to awe.

If spirituality never moves to religion, it stays stunted, stays on training wheels. But whichever religion it moves to must be seen, in some sense, as an incomplete and provisional answer to the enigma of the divine. No religion, after all, can either say or understand everything about God because humans ultimately cannot comprehend the infinite. Which is not to say that all religions are the same or that all religious ideas are of equal value. Some religious ideas—such as the idea that airplanes should be flown into skyscrapers to defend religion and promote it—are, in fact, of far less than zero value, as was confirmed for my family in the 9/11 terrorist attacks in which my nephew died as a passenger on the first plane to slam into the World Trade Center.

> True spirituality has to do with awe, with wonder, with an openness to the inexplicable beauty of the creation and its creatures.

This inadequacy of religion to understand everything about the divine is precisely the point at which we must turn to faith, or trust. I will not use the overused, dismissive term "blind faith" because that implies an unreasonable faith, a faith that hasn't burrowed its way through shadows and storms of doubt, a faith that asks little or nothing of its holder. Blind faith might be considered cheap faith in the same way that German Lutheran martyr Dietrich Bonhoeffer employed the term "cheap grace" to refer to a gift that requires nothing of us in return.[14]

I think the best place for people to wind up on a spiritual journey is to keep the sense of awe and wonder that characterizes spirituality even while having some answers from religion about causes—answers that are satisfying enough to make one want to continue to live in harmony with the creation and its inhabitants.

> If spirituality never moves to religion, it stays stunted, stays on training wheels.

When I say "wind up on a spiritual journey," I mean nothing of the sort, of course. If you "wind up" somewhere, the journey is over and the questioning comes to an end. It's one reason we must never stop talking about all matters of spirituality, religion, and faith, for once we stop talking we might actually believe the last thing we said.

LET'S TALK ABOUT THIS

What's the most interesting spiritual question you ever asked or ever heard asked? Did you find any answers to it?

What almost always gives you a sense of awe and wonder? Is that sense enough to still your questions about faith or do you need more? Explain.

Can you really be religious but not spiritual?

No doubt something like fundamentalism has infected faith ever since humans first felt the religious impulse. By fundamentalism I mean a false certitude about eternal things, a rigid approach to all religious matters that leaves no room for doubt or debate, no space where humility might dwell, no awareness that other sincere people have arrived at different answers, or at least no tolerance for those answers. There is a desperation about such fundamentalism that I find terribly unattractive.

I am tempted to call people with this disease religious but not spiritual, though perhaps that's an insult to both religious and spiritual people. But if religion has lost its capacity for wonder, for awe, and is, instead, stuck with nothing but indisputable creedal formulations, it has become a serious detriment to civilization.

In this sense, I have had two close associations with people I would call religious but not spiritual. The first are the Branch Davidians, whose home, Mount Carmel, near Waco, Texas, burned to the ground in 1993 after the group had a long standoff with federal authorities. The result was the unnecessary loss of

> By fundamentalism I mean a false certitude about eternal things, a rigid approach to all religious matters that leaves no room for doubt or debate, no space where humility might dwell.

many lives—four of them law enforcement authorities and more than eighty of them Branch Davidians, among them their leader, David Koresh.

I went to Waco the next year to try to analyze what had gone wrong. The result was a series of analyses I wrote for the *Kansas City Star*—articles reprinted in my previously mentioned first book, *A Gift of Meaning*. Some of my conclusions:

> There's an important lesson to be learned here on this Texas pasture land and killing field—a lesson our government violently failed to grasp: In the United States we protect people with strange religious beliefs, we don't assault them.... At Waco, our government ignored both its constitutional and its spiritual roots. It unleashed on a deeply religious—if strange and misguided—people the repressive, coercive, violent power of the state. Then its representatives lied about what happened. Then they tried to hide what happened by issuing reports that reeked of deceit. The government's failure—built on hostility toward religious freedom—was both widespread and deep, finally reaching all the way to the Oval Office, where President Clinton, when informed of the plan to gas the Branch Davidians, first failed to demand the highest standard of constitutional protection for people of faith and then compounded his failure with post-fire dismissive rhetoric that stained and cheapened his office.[15]

One of the saddest failures of the government in the Branch Davidian affair was that right in Waco, at Baylor University, there were religious experts who had studied the Davidians over the several decades that this group had lived in that area and who could have warned authorities not to take the actions they wound up taking, if only these scholars had been consulted. But federal officials didn't bother to talk with those experts. Instead, they blundered their way to a deadly disaster.

Many documents recording negotiations between federal officials and Branch Davidian leaders reveal a deeply contemptuous attitude toward people whom the feds considered religious but not spiritual, which is to say that they thought of them as religious nuts, whacked-out cult members who could not find a way to fit into American culture. Through long and careful reading—as well as many interviews with people on all sides of this matter, including surviving Davidians—I concluded that the Davidians were, in fact, way out of any mainstream of religion. Yet that was no reason for their lives to end the way they did. There were proper ways to effect the arrest of Koresh and any other Davidians suspected of arms violations and even of child abuse. The courts could have sorted out what was true and what wasn't. That—and not thunderous attack—is the American system.

> I wish I knew what would prevent people from moving into a state in which they lose their spiritual bearings and become, instead, religious automatons.

It's clear that, in some cases, being religious but not spiritual in the United States can get you into trouble with authorities who take it upon themselves not simply to enforce the law but also to enforce cultural prejudices and norms.

The other religious but not spiritual group that smashed into my life was the collection of 9/11 al-Qaida terrorists who hid behind Islam that malevolent day to justify murdering some three thousand people, including the only son of one of my sisters and her husband. Karleton D. B. Fyfe was a passenger on the first plane, American flight no. 11, to crash into the World Trade Center that morning. He was thirty-one years old, married, the father of a toddler, and had just learned that his and Haven's second child was due in May 2002. Karleton was a bond analyst for John Hancock and was on his way to a business meeting in Los Angeles. He and I were quite close and not a day goes by even now when I don't think of him and miss him.

The Islamist terrorists who, at the urging of the late Osama bin Laden, pulled off this spectacularly evil deed had abandoned anything like spirituality in favor of a vision of religion that required assent to cockamamie ideas unworthy of any major world religion. The misuse of the Qur'an and the *hadith* (the collections of sayings and actions of the Prophet Muhammad) was and continues to be monumental and outrageous among these and similar theological thugs. Taken to an almost unimaginable extreme, it's what can happen when religion becomes devoid of the spirit, awe, wonder, and humility of healthy faith.

I wish I knew what would prevent people from moving into a state in which they lose their spiritual bearings and become, instead, religious automatons, willing to blow airplanes out of the sky, murder cartoonists, behead captives, cage captured pilots and burn them alive, and die themselves in a misguided attempt at martyrdom. All I know to do is to try to help people understand what healthy faith looks like, feels like, is. That is why I have written this book, though, of course, I know it will not be enough.

NEAR WACO, APRIL 19, 1993

When the children first smelled the smoke,
first heard
the dry rush of fire
run amok,
fire eating the edges of their pinched world,
their sad, unhinged, indecent place,
did their hearts,
their tiny fibrillating hearts,
say to them what, on so many stark nights,
they must have feared—
that in this world
there is no love for them?

LET'S TALK ABOUT THIS

Do you know people you would describe as religious but not spiritual? What do you find attractive about that and what do you find repellant?

If you are old enough to remember, what do you recall about your immediate reaction to the Branch Davidian deaths in 1993 and the terrorist attacks of September 11, 2001? Were you angry at God? If so, how did you express that anger?

Why are we so afraid of uncertainty?

In high school and college I was attracted to physics because of its ability to offer some fascinating guesses about how the world works. I eventually discovered that to do physics one should have at least minimal math skills, whereas my talents in that area were always subpar (and have remained consistently so). As people with my low level of ability with numbers say, "There are three kinds of people in the world—those with math skills and those without math skills." Thus, I did what many people without math skills do—I went into journalism. Do not trust, but always doubt, math answers offered to you by any journalist, even business reporters. Fair warning. Faith in numbers from such a source is misplaced.

Despite all that, I have retained a profound attraction to both big-end and little-end physics, which is to say to cosmology and to subatomic physics, or quantum mechanics—and have written a fair amount about both over the years. One reason is that I have come to appreciate the implications in both science, and the rest of life, of Werner Heisenberg's Uncertainty Principle, first proposed in 1927, a little over a decade after Albert Einstein introduced his Theory of General Relativity, and just a few years after Karl Barth's transformative commentary on the New Testament book of Romans was published.[16] (I'll try to connect those two developments eventually here—and may fail.)

The Uncertainty Principle essentially says that if you're dealing with subatomic particles, the more precisely you know the location of one, the less precisely you can know the speed at which it's traveling.

And, of course, the more precisely you know the speed of it, the less precisely you can know where it is. (This may have marked the beginning of postmodernism, with its rejection of previously accepted meta-narratives and its sometimes-overenthusiastic embrace of ambiguity.) So, you can never know both location and speed at the same time with any useful accuracy. This conclusion did not result from what became known as the observer effect—the idea that it is impossible to observe something in the subatomic world without affecting it. Rather, the Uncertainty Principle is baked into reality. It is an acknowledgment that the universe is full of mystery, of what to our wondering eyes looks like imprecision, randomness, chance, wildness—what I think of as what-the-hellness.

> Those of us grounded in the biblical witness and in our appreciation for metaphor, myth, and allegory know that all of life has been marinated in uncertainty from the beginning.

Once people began to grasp the slippery nature of reality, all the way down to quarks and antiquarks, to say nothing of gluons, all bets were off. What, after all, could really be known for certain? How could any measurement, any observation be trustworthy? We really didn't know what we thought we knew. A scary imprecision had forced itself upon us and we would forever be unable to see reality in the same way, though many people, stuck in a Newtonian world, continue to try, even today.

People of faith should not have been shocked by the Uncertainty Principle (or Einstein's theory of relativity) or its unnerving implications in and beyond science. Those of us grounded in the biblical witness and in our appreciation for metaphor, myth, and allegory know that all of life has been marinated in uncertainty from the beginning. After all, breath—God's breath, especially when mixed with dust to yield humanity—tends toward that lack of fixedness. The wind, as even Jesus noted, blows where it will.

The Franciscan priest and writer Richard Rohr expressed this reality especially well in his book *Falling Upward*:

Life, as the biblical tradition makes clear, is both loss and renewal, death and resurrection, chaos and healing at the same time; life seems to be a collision of opposites.... Most of us were formed by Newtonian worldviews in which everything had a clear cause and effect, what might be called an "if-then" worldview. All causality was clear and defined. The truth we are now beginning to respect is that the universe seems to proceed through a web of causes, just as human motivation does, producing ever-increasing diversity, multiplicity, dark holes, dark matter, death and rebirth, loss and renewal in different forms, and yes even violence, the continual breaking of the rules of "reason" that make wise people look for more all-embracing rules and a larger "logic." Nature is much more disorder than order, more multiplicity than uniformity, with the greatest disorder being death itself! In the spiritual life, and now in science, we learn much more by honoring and learning from the exceptions than by just imposing our previous certain rules to make everything fit.[17]

Our love of pattern and design, our preference for certainty, our one-then-two-then-three nature makes it terribly difficult for us to be comfortable with the sort of ambiguity Rohr says is found in the biblical tradition or the uncertainty that Heisenberg described in quantum mechanics. We experience chaos but seem resistant to it—so resistant, in fact, that we deny the chaos or cover it with some unifying principle that declares all people sinful from birth or that limits the possible ways God may be discovered and revealed or that insists that only these words and not those can adequately describe eternal matters. We want the stories that play out in front of our eyes to fit the categories we've already created for them in our compartmentalized brains. So we wind up distorting some of those stories and missing their points because, in fact, a kind of universal Uncertainty Principle is in operation that prevents us from knowing both the historically verifiable details of a story and the many possible meanings of that story. We can never get all that together perfectly. Life is messy, moving, slippery, and unwilling to change just because we want everything to match up with the universal standards we imagine to exist. Yet, Pultizer Prize–winning essayist Marilynne Robinson is right when she says, "There are worse things than uncertainty, presumption being one."[18]

In the mid- and late 1800s, what came to be known as liberal theology spread among American Christian leaders, especially those connected to some theological seminaries. One idea the liberals promoted was that Jesus Christ was a model for the culture more than he was a universal savior. And, they said, by following this model each of us might somehow move closer to perfection. After World War I's brutality disabused many of the planet's residents of the idea that humans were perfectible, the disenchanted poet Ezra Pound wrote in his poem "Hugh Selwyn Mauberley" that lots of people died "For an old bitch gone in the teeth, for a botched civilization."[19]

Into this profound postwar disillusionment came Barth with his commentary on Romans in which he essentially argued that the liberals, the Jesus-as-mostly-a-model people, had it wrong and that we needed to return to the shocking, radical call of the gospel to engage the messy world with the idea that truth can never be found in doctrines or dogma or in the culture but only in Jesus Christ, God incarnate. By arguing for what became known as neo-orthodoxy, Barth was affirming that what Christianity has to offer is what Rohr has called biblically recorded "loss and renewal, death and resurrection, chaos and healing at the same time." Yes, it was offering that, along with the hope—the sweet, sweet hope even when (and maybe only when) we feel God has abandoned us—that God in Christ, as he promised in Matthew 28:20, will be "with you always, even to the end of the age" (NLT). Christianity never promised inevitable human progress, or redemption of the culture by human ideas and ingenuity. There was and is only the gospel, the good

> Christianity never promised inevitable human progress, or redemption of the culture by human ideas and ingenuity.

news that the reign of God is breaking into the world right now and we can experience it today in light of the news that the resurrection of Jesus has changed everything.

If that's not enough for faith formation, maybe nothing is.

LET'S TALK ABOUT THIS

Did you ever feel a calling to a profession or hobby for which you discovered you had no skills? If so, what was it? Did you rethink whether that was just a whim or, in fact, a divine calling that you didn't follow through far enough to see where it might take you?

When, if ever, do you feel as if the reign, or kingdom, of God that Jesus said was at hand is, in fact, breaking in? Is it in any way your job to speed up its flowering? If so, how?

Why must faith keep asking questions?

In 2014 I came back onto my church's Session, or board of elders, to fill out the one-year term of an elder who had left the job early. For that year, I chaired the Faith Development Committee, which oversees our adult education offerings.

And all that year I was (and remain) a bit uncomfortable with the term "faith development." It seems to imply an inexorable progress, a straight line from ignorance to enlightenment. But we know that's not how things work. Spiritual growth is an up-and-down, often erratic business. We have an epiphany today and then for neither love nor money can we remember tomorrow what it was. Or we commit ourselves to a particular understanding of this or that passage of scripture, or this or that approach to faith, and then realize a few years down the road that we've thrown most of that over and have moved in a different direction.

Faith is fluid and cannot be otherwise if it is alive.

My own path of faith began as a regular Sunday school attender at First Presbyterian Church of Woodstock, Illinois. This Mainline Protestant atmosphere tended to encourage questions—except, as I will explain later, among young teens, whose questions the adults seemed unprepared to answer—and conversation, but also adherence to the core of traditional Christianity. As I left high school—if not a little before—I drifted away on purpose, certain that I did not want to be connected with all the hypocrites I found in church. I remained essentially unchurched for about a dozen years, though in all that time I never lost my hunger for answers to the everlasting questions about life and its purpose. So while I was drifting, I did things like attend lay theology courses at Colgate-Rochester Divinity School while working at my first postcollege job at the *Times-Union*, the now-defunct afternoon newspaper in Rochester, New York.

Eventually, this intentional distance from a faith community began to feel like an ill fit, and my then-wife and I, by then parents of two little girls, began to find our way back to church. It helped that I finally recognized that I was one of the hypocrites. Not long after I joined Second Presbyterian Church of Kansas City, Missouri, in 1978, I was asked to help teach a sixth- and seventh-grade Sunday school class and to serve on the Board of Deacons, which in Presbyterian polity is an elected position, as is the office of elder. It turns out that, if you intend to teach children, you need to know more than they do and to be able to explain faith in ways that make sense to them. So I began to read theology and related material in a way that was even more intentional than when I was a floater.

> Faith is fluid and cannot be otherwise if it is alive.

Over the years, under the influence of this pastor or that, of this author or that, of this movement or that, I have occupied what I think of as Christianity's broad theological middle—sometimes leaning more to the right, sometimes more to the left, but always within what most Christians would recognize as a "generous orthodoxy," the term emerging church movement guru Brian McLaren attached to it in his book of that title.[20] What I have never been, either as a child, a youth, or an adult is a fundamentalist, a literalist, a theological ideologue. I have come to believe that such a path is the way to destructive misunderstandings and, finally, intellectual and spiritual dishonesty, atrophy, and chaos. Such a path forecloses questions and serious conversation in favor of answers approved by certain authorities. And, as I say, I think unanswered questions are better than unquestioned answers.

True faith cannot survive in an atmosphere in which answers are unquestioned. It's not that at some point you don't settle, at least temporarily, on an answer to this or that question. But even then it helps to remember that there may yet be more light to shine on the matter. If you are holding fast to theological answers you first learned or articulated when you were six or twenty-five or fifty and you're now seventy or eighty, you've spent your life on a spiritual treadmill and I am sorry about that (though what Billy Crystal's character said of himself and his friends in the film *City Slickers*—a quote also attributed to Yogi Berra and others—may be true of you: "We're lost, but we're making good time"). But it's never too late to rejoin the conversation, to reenlist in the school of the mind and the heart, to reattach yourself to a living faith that moves in harmony with the living God. In fact, you can begin today.

> True faith cannot survive in an atmosphere in which answers are unquestioned.

LET'S TALK ABOUT THIS

If you drew a diagram of your spiritual journey so far, what would it look like?

Do you have a regular opportunity to ask hard questions about religion with people who help you find at least provisional answers? If not, how might you create that kind of community?

So why is doubt
so valuable?

I have danced around the question of doubt a bit so far in this book. Undoubtedly it's time to confront it more directly.

Healthy faith is impossible without doubt—at least a faith that can find its sea legs and survive the inevitable theological, personal, social, and cultural storms it will encounter. Doubt is what drives us to ask dangerous questions, to challenge previously unquestioned answers. Doubt is what clears away the religious debris that masquerades as truth, forcing doubters to rethink, to analyze, to discern, to pray, to search for a way home until, finally, they submit to the overwhelming, astonishing, loving presence we call God. (More about that in a moment.) As religion professor Jacqueline A. Bussie says in her book *Outlaw Christian: Finding Authentic Faith by Breaking the "Rules,"* "Doubt is a sign of a healthy and deep-rooted faith, though most of us are taught to believe the opposite."[21]

The opposite of faith is not doubt. The opposite of faith is certitude. Doubt creates the space in which faith may live. Certitude kills faith. It turns faith into a rigid caricature of itself, a Madame Tussauds' wax figure of the real thing. It may, from a distance, look genuine, but no real blood runs through it. There is no health in it. As much as its holders might pretend that it is vibrant, it is, in fact, comatose. Twentieth-century Protestant theologian Paul Tillich put it this

> The opposite of faith is not doubt. The opposite of faith is certitude.

way: "Sometimes I think it is my mission to bring faith to the faithless, and doubt to the faithful."[22]

The story of Job in the Hebrew Scriptures is not, in the end, a story about doubt. Rather, it's a story about the certitude of Job's friends (whom I call the biblical Three Stooges), Eliphaz the Temanite, Bildad the Shuhite, and Zophar the Naamathite. These guys had all the answers for why Job was being plagued with trouble. "Here's your problem," they'd say, in effect, and then they'd lay out a line of bad, if common, theology that suggested suffering was a sign that someone had sinned. The remarkable thing about the book of Job is that it challenged the conventional wisdom about suffering on that score—and it did so persuasively.

> It is only when we are free to confront God with our doubts, to demand that God be God, as promised, that we have a chance to fly into the open arms of this God.

But notice what happens at the end of the story (just don't rush to get there). Job, who has maintained his innocence throughout (and not very patiently), is brought into the presence of the living God. This God does not answer all of Job's challenging questions about why bad things happen to good people. Rather, once Job experiences being in God's presence, his questions are silenced. He no longer needs answers. His answer is God's healing presence itself, which calms the waters and gives Job a chance to acknowledge that "I was talking about things I knew nothing about, things far too wonderful for me." Job, in God's presence, discovers and embraces humility.

Burton Z. Cooper, a former professor at Louisville Presbyterian Theological Seminary, opened my eyes to this in a piece he wrote in 1986 for the journal *Theology Today*. He wrote:

> Job is healed when a new image of God appears to him. Now he can let go of the monarchial image of God. He is healed because, in letting go of the image of all-controlling power, he is letting go of the experience

of God as the enemy, the one who "crushes" him. The "thee" that he sees in "now my eye sees thee" is God the friend, the vulnerable one, who is there with him in his suffering and whose caring presence heals him. He does not repent of his concern for God's justice; biblical faith can never have enough of that concern. Job repents of his loathing for life, his sense of despair, his lack of faith in the goodness of the creation. Thus, he is ready to return to life. He can love again, work, and have children. He can die, as the text says, "full of days."[23]

The kind of resolute doubt Job went through is the path toward the humility and faith he eventually embraced. We must, in fact, express our doubts, raise our angry questions about why God would permit hurricanes to kill small children, about why God did not stop Adolf Hitler's Nazi killing machine before it had exterminated some six million Jews, two-thirds of the Jews of Europe. It is only when we are free to confront God with our doubts, to demand that God be God, as promised, that we have a chance to fly into the open arms of this God and to realize that we, too, were asking about things we knew nothing about, things too wonderful for us.

> Certitude is a tool of evil. Doubt, by contrast, is the road toward epiphany, enlightenment, an acknowledgment that God is God and we are not.

That's when we can become aware of the astonishing, healing presence of God and of our assurance, as Julian of Norwich put it, that "all shall be well, and all shall be well, and all manner of things shall be well."

In the course of my life of faith, I have doubted almost everything that has to do with religion: God, biblical stories, love, and even whether life has purpose and meaning. I am not out of the ordinary in this way. It's a common human experience—even among the children of harsh fundamentalists in various religious traditions who discourage doubt and term it a tool of the devil. But that attitude gets

> To avoid doubt is, in the end, to avoid finding such a faith.

it exactly backwards. Certitude is a tool of evil. Doubt, by contrast, is the road toward epiphany, enlightenment, an acknowledgment that God is God and we are not. It's the road toward a rich faith. To avoid doubt is, in the end, to avoid finding such a faith.

As the late Christian author and teacher Dallas Willard writes, "Many churchgoers have been taught not to question what they hear in church and that doubt is a bad thing. But they are missing the great value of doubt—it can stimulate you to keep thinking and asking questions."[24] Thinking and asking questions—that's what I call faithful living.

LET'S TALK ABOUT THIS

Do you value doubt or do you do everything you can to avoid it? If the latter, do you end up with doubts anyway? How do you handle them?

How often, if at all, do you reexamine your long-held religious beliefs? How often do you think you *should* reexamine them?

Does it help to compare religions?

One of the inevitable questions about religion is whether one faith tradition is just as good as another. That question and its implicit criticism (or at least dismissal) of faith traditions generally is what the poet T. S. Eliot, in "The Love Song of J. Alfred Prufrock," calls a "tedious argument of insidious intent."[25] Which is to say that it is asked by people who already know what answer they would give—and, indeed, are ready to give it, whether it's asked for or not.

For many people who identify themselves as adherents of no religion, the answer is obvious: Yes, all religions are roughly the same (you can pretty much boil them down to the Golden Rule) and none of the exclusivist claims each one makes is persuasive. For many people who are passionate followers of a particular religion, the answer is also obvious: No, my religion is best because it's the faith that God has deemed the only truth. There's also a group of people who believe there are many paths to the top of the same mountain and that it mostly doesn't make any difference which path you choose because, if you are persistent, you will reach God eventually—or God will reach you.

I'm not fond of any of those positions. But that, frankly, doesn't leave me much room to maneuver between and among certitude, wishy-washiness, inclusive nonselectiveness, and a commitment that is both deep and wide. Still, the place where I want to stand is one that allows me to be profoundly and eternally committed to the broad center of Christianity (and, thus, to Christ) while at the same time one that requires me to be respectful of the many choices that others make outside of that tradition.

Several years ago I had a lengthy conversation with Rabbi Brad Hirschfield, nationally renowned Jewish leader and author, about this very issue.[26] He said some things that have been helpful to me as I try to find a place to stand that allows me to keep my own commitment to Christianity while not disparaging other religions in an age when good interfaith relations may be the key to a peaceful world. Hirschfield told me:

> More often than not what we call interfaith dialogue is really interfaithless. People from nominal commitments to a tradition come together to overtly affirm some general stuff that they would have agreed to anyway even if they weren't in the same room. It's insulting, actually. Real interfaith dialogue is hard. And until you know you've experienced its hard edge, you're not there. Until you've experienced something at risk, you're not there. And until the other side is ready to be present to you even when they don't like what they're hearing, you're not there.
>
> In Jewish life, by and large, the deeper I go, the narrower I get. So what happens in interfaith settings is—this sounds harsh—that the people have the shallowest or the least base of knowledge. I'm not saying intent or faith or interest, but the shallowest base of knowledge. And they're able to be very broad because of it. Most times, at least in Jewish life, when someone gets a hold of someone and deepens their Jewishness, it's amazing. The rest of the world falls away. We actually haven't figured out yet how to prepare people to be both deep and wide.
>
> Right now we have very few people who combine deep passion and commitment with genuine openness. That for me is the mandate. The open people find themselves incapable of committing to anything and the committed people are so terrified of the commitments

> others make that they shut down almost immediately.
> Genuine commitment and deep openness is the man-
> date of living in the presence of one God who is infi-
> nite, because I know I'm finite. I have to deeply, deeply,
> deeply commit to what I have in front of me and then
> be very honest that it's one little part of something
> much bigger.

The key here is to recognize what I've described earlier: the finite nature of the human mind that seeks to grasp the infinite. Early Protestant reformer John Calvin put it this way: "[H]ow can the human mind ... under its own guidance, penetrate to a knowledge of the substance of God while unable to understand its own?"[27] The internationally renowned Christian artist Makoto Fujimura makes a similar point in describing the work of Japanese Catholic author Shusaku Endo: "... modernist reductionism ... entirely rejects doubt—as if we, in our limited minds and knowledge, can know everything God and the universe offer to us."[28]

The night before I wrote the first draft of this section of this book, I attended a meditation group in the San Francisco Bay Area that has been important to my oldest sister, who lives in Berkeley (I have three sisters but no brothers). The readings for the evening were steeped in the Hindu tradition, though the spirit of the group clearly was open to the idea that there are many valuable and effective spiritual paths. I was struck by how this small group of adults—most of whom were at or past retirement age—was continuing to struggle with the eternal questions, continuing to entertain new ideas about God and faith, and continuing to rely on such ancient sacred writings as the Upanishads for wisdom and insight.

Had there been opportunity for sharing our different religious experiences and commitments, I might have been moved to say a word about why being a disciple of Jesus Christ has brought me both immense challenge and deep joy. I may have told them that I wish for them a similar experience and I may have invited them to find a way to meet this subversive Jesus, whom I attempt to follow. But the evening wasn't structured for such a conversation, so all I could do was appreciate the reality that each person there was a seeker. Including me, of course.

One of the reasons it's important to get interfaith relations on the right track these days is that the religious landscape in the United States has shifted fairly dramatically since 1965, when President Lyndon B. Johnson signed immigration reform into law.[29] The result of that was an influx of new citizens from all over the world, but especially from Asia, Africa, and the Southern Hemisphere, people who brought with them their Hinduism, Islam, Jainism, Buddhism, and many other faiths, including versions of Christianity rather new to our American shores. As that influx has occurred, the percentage of Americans identifying as religiously unaffiliated has risen and now may be up to about 23 percent of the adult population. As I've written elsewhere often, if the call of the twentieth century to Americans was to get race relations right (still very much a work in progress), the call of the twenty-first century is to get interfaith relations right. The benefits of doing that are obvious and impressive, including community harmony and respectful understanding of our neighbors. The dangers of not doing that are also obvious but frightening, including ignorance, misunderstanding, prejudice, and even violence.

Healthy faith leaves room not just for doubt but also for the different experiences of others. Healthy faith, as the Apostle Paul said of love, does not insist on its own way, but it does make its way clear for others to see, so they may evaluate it and follow it if they want to or feel called to. People of faith can say, with Martin Luther, "Here I stand. I can do no other...." But they also can respect people who say the same thing from a different position—unless, of course, that position means that they seek to destroy anyone who doesn't believe as they do. (I'm looking at you, Islamist terrorists, among others.)

Is one religion just as good as another? The answer is the same as the answer to this question: Are all ideas of equal value? Of course not. But before we decide what value an idea or a religion has, we are required to study the matter in detail, including getting to know people who are committed to that religion or idea. Only then will our response be genuine and worth hearing.

LET'S TALK ABOUT THIS

Do you think all religions are pretty much the same, equally meaningless; that one is God-ordained and, thus, best and right; or that there are many valid paths to God? Or is there another choice? Explain your thoughts.

What experience have you had engaging in some kind of interfaith dialogue or similar contact? What did it teach you?

TAKING DOUBT
SERIOUSLY

Are 9-1-1 prayers for help the most genuine kind?

Before every meal in our house when I was a boy—well, except breakfast, which tended to be a disorganized, you're-on-your-own sort of affair—the six of us said this grace:

> "Dear Lord, bless this food to our use and us to thy service. Amen."

Our food did not go from hot to cold while we said it. But its brevity was a clue to the thinness of its theological content. The "Lord" apparently didn't have a name, not even The Name, which is what Jews mean when they pray to or talk about *HaShem*. We apparently assumed that we meant Christianity's triune God, though more likely most of us around the table thought of Jesus whenever we said the word "Lord," though why Jesus and not God the Father was putting food on our table was never explained. (It turned out later that I understood Jesus himself to be food. Imagine that.)

The prayer also was a demand or command to whoever this Lord was: Bless this food. We did not say, "We ask that you bless this food" or "Please bless this food." No, it was a directive to the power of the cosmos from six Middle American Presbyterians having lunch or dinner around an oaken, oval-shaped table in the big kitchen of the old 1883 home we bought in 1948 and kept in the family for nearly fifty years.[1] The prayer was presumptuous, of course, but it helped us think that we were being grateful to someone besides ourselves for food that we had either grown in our garden or bought in a grocery store. (And, at the end, our prayer of grace partly rescued itself by reminding us of our duty to serve.)

A lot of prayer is presumptuous and directive—especially 9-1-1 prayers for help in the midst of crisis, those prayers that are shot-gunned out into the empty air by anxious people who may not have prayed in years. Yet, in some ways, they are the most genuine, the most human of prayers. They arise from our muddled, frightened, feeling-betrayed depths—as did Jesus's own prayer from the cross in the opening line of Psalm 22: "My God, my God, why have you forsaken me?" (KJV). They seek some destination that might at minimum be benign and at most be loving or at least attentive. There may well be atheists in foxholes, but even some of them have been known to issue forlorn pleas that begin, "O God ..."

> A lot of prayer is presumptuous and directive—especially 9-1-1 prayers for help in the midst of crisis.

Yet many of us are shaped by the prayers of our childhood—all the "God bless Mommy, God bless Daddy" pleas children heave toward the heavens. The old bedtime prayer, for instance, that somehow morbidly (if realistically) anticipates the death of a child in the midst of sleep—"if I should die before I wake"—was useful for reminding us of life's fragile nature and of the inevitability of death, which many people in our death-denying culture now seem to think is optional.

But those words about dying in the night preceded a plea that in many ways was profoundly un-Christian in its assumed theology: "I pray the Lord my soul to take." Although not stating it directly, these words seemed to hint at a theological dualism that separates body and soul, something Judaism and Christianity refuse to do. Traditional Christianity—save when it goes astray, as it does in parts of the 1647 Protestant Reformation creed, the Westminster Confession of Faith, on this point—does not teach that we have an immortal soul and that the soul will, at the moment of death, escape from our now-useful and -battered body (although you can hear that soul-departure theology a lot at Christian funerals and at funeral home calling hours).[2] The idea of an immortal soul is an old Greek one, not a Christian one. The Christian alternative is the doctrine of the resurrection of the body.

As the late theologian and teacher Shirley C. Guthrie Jr., writes in his excellent book *Christian Doctrine:*

> The belief in the immortality of the soul ... was not taught by the biblical writers themselves, but it was common in the Greek and Oriental religions of the ancient world in which the Christian church was born.... [But] if we hold to the genuinely biblical hope for the future, we must firmly reject this doctrine of the soul's immortality ... [t]he Christian hope is not in the indestructibility of man, but in the creative power of God.[3]

It turns out that only God is immortal, not us. If God wants us to spend eternity in the divine presence, that's up to God. Seems simple enough, but I'm frequently astonished at how this grace-based, God-based approach to faith is superseded by a theology that locates humanity at the center, a pattern first established in the Adam and Eve story.

However, as I say, at least the short grace we said before meals got the service-to-others part right. Implicit in that "us to thy service" wording are Jesus's own shocking words from Matthew 25:40: "when you have done it for one of the least of these brothers and sisters of mine, you have done it for me" (CEB).

> The idea of an immortal soul is an old Greek one, not a Christian one. The Christian alternative is the doctrine of the resurrection of the body.

Which, of course, requires of us perhaps the most difficult part of faith: to see Christ in everyone else, from the dying wretch to the plumber to the first lady to the pope. It's an inhuman task, which is what makes it so human.

LET'S TALK ABOUT THIS

What's the closest you've come to crying out to God with a 9-1-1 emergency prayer? Did you find it answered in some way or did you experience silence? Explain.

Do distinctions between the old Greek idea of the immortality of the soul and the Christian doctrine of the resurrection of the body make any difference to you? If so, in what way? Or does that just feel like discussing how many angels can dance on the head of a pin?

If you're Christian, do you agree that seeing Christ in other people is the most difficult part of faith or is there something else even harder? If so, what is it?

What if we fail to take our children's faith questions seriously?

It was toward the end of seventh grade that my family moved back to Woodstock, Illinois, after two years in India. Seventh grade is full of prodigies and idiots, the maturing and the never-will-mature, sensible children and kids who would eat live worms just to say they'd done it. And this is all pretty much the same child, depending on the day of the week and the time of day.

On Sunday mornings of my seventh-grade Sunday school year at First Presbyterian Church of Woodstock, a dozen or so kids—mostly boys, as I recall; maybe all boys—sat around a table in a corner of the multipurpose room that had been added to the church a few years earlier. Only we didn't exactly just sit there. We degenerated into the habit of laughing, talking, making jokes, poking each other, making faces—in short, driving our teacher absolutely daft. I say "our teacher," but the sad truth was that over the course of a year or so, which must have included some or all of eighth grade, too, we mowed down seven different teachers. Count 'em: seven. They found us simply incorrigible and left us.

> Our teachers did not take our juvenile minds seriously enough.

We were inexplicably relentless, uncontrollable, manic almost. I still cannot quite explain what happened to us. But over the years I've developed a theory, drawn partly from my own later experience of teaching sixth- and seventh-grade Sunday school for several years. My theory is that our teachers did not take our juvenile minds seriously enough. They did not anticipate the fact that we already were beginning to think abstractly and to ask—at least to ourselves—eternal questions rooted in our earliest doubts about faith. Those teachers seemed stuck with some kind of denominational curriculum that encouraged nonabstract answers to complex questions and eventually we knew we would not have our deepest longings for insight and comfort answered in ways that would matter to us. (Either that or we were just jerks. No, really. That might have been it.)

No doubt some enterprising scholar could have earned a nice doctorate studying why we slid into a sort of *Lord of the Flies* situation at that corner table on Sunday mornings. It almost made one believe in Original Sin. But, as I say, the reality was that we had questions we didn't know how to ask and we had essentially untrained teachers who may not have known how to respond even if we had asked them. So we abandoned ship and went with junior high noncriminal delinquency.

One of the sad truths about faith traditions is that not many adherents of them know how to pass along the faith to their children in ways that respond to the child's developmental state while also serving the tradition's long-term interests and future. We Christians tell toddlers that Jesus loves them and this news pretty well suffices until they approach their teenage years, by which time they have seen enough cognitive dissonance in life to begin to question everything. At that point, some branches of Christianity simply try to scare young people into adopting the essential tenets of the faith by talking about a wrathful God and hell (accounting for the widespread, misguided popularity of the penal substitutionary atonement theory),[4] while other branches opt for what theology teacher Kenda Creasy Dean, in her book *Almost Christian: What the Faith of Our Teenagers Is Telling the American Church*, has popularized as the notion of "moralistic therapeutic deism."[5]

> One of the sad truths about faith traditions is that not many adherents of them know how to pass along the faith to their children.

Essentially that means that God just wants you to be nice and won't bother you much if you at least try to achieve that modest goal.

Both are irresponsible ways to teach children. One cuts off important questions; the other cuts off important answers.

There certainly are capable youth leaders and teachers in almost all faith traditions who are engaging young people thoughtfully and guiding them toward a faith they can embrace with enthusiasm, even if they are left with unanswered questions. What is crucial to remember at this point—and throughout a life of faith—is that unanswered questions are always better than unquestioned answers because the former keep the search going. But the decline of Mainline Protestant churches stands as stark testimony to the reality that many churches don't handle any of this well. And once young people abandon faith, it takes an enormous effort and a different set of skills and approaches to reengage them.

> Unanswered questions are always better than unquestioned answers because the former keep the search going.

I long for children to experience the embracing love of a faith community that cherishes them and wants to take them and their questions seriously. In retrospect, I even long to be back in seventh grade at that table in the church in Woodstock with a teacher who would grab us by the heart and the cerebrum and point us toward eternal questions and doubts that we would be required to struggle with for the rest of our lives.

Instead, at least for a year, we got wet willies and belches.

LET'S TALK ABOUT THIS

If you attended Sunday school as a child, did you come away with wonderful memories of a favorite teacher or did the experience sour you on faith? Why?

As a child, did you have someone trustworthy in your life whom you could seek out for answers to faith questions? How can you be such a person for other children today?

When are words and silence sacred?

Words are sacred. No, wait. Words *can* be sacred but aren't always so. As part of a series of *Kansas City Star* columns I did about the four seasons, I once wrote words about the purposes of autumn. A mother from Centralia, Illinois, later wrote to tell me that she had asked someone to read those words at the grave of her teenage son on the day he was buried. Those were sacred words in that they comforted the bereaved. I once wrote a column for the *National Catholic Reporter* that was an open letter to Pope Francis asking that he remove Kansas City Bishop Robert W. Finn because he had criminally failed to protect children in his diocese from an abusive priest.[6] Those were sacred words in that they defended the most vulnerable. And I once wrote (with my friend Rabbi Jacques Cukierkorn) a book that told stories about non-Jews who saved Jews in the Holocaust in Poland.[7] If those words weren't sacred, at least they pointed to sacred acts.

The witness of the Bible, of course, is that God spoke the world into existence. By definition, any words God uses are sacred. "Let there be light" may, in fact, be the most generative sacred words ever spoken, though each time I read them or hear them I continue to wonder who heard them and wrote them down—and in what language. It's just the kind of question a person of faith should ask. The fact that there's no answer to it—at least none we can know—confirms that by asking it we're on the right track, for it moves us to that humbling cloud of unknowing.[8]

The Hebrew tradition honors words by acknowledging their astonishing power not just to create the world but also to re-create it, to change the path of history, to participate in the process of creation. As I've said, this respect for words is one reason that when Jews today speak of God, they often use the term *HaShem*, which simply means The Name. In this view, the name of God is so powerful and sacred that one should never be so presumptuous as to utter it or write it out. That's why you see some Jews writing about God but not spelling the word out fully, so it becomes, in English, "G-d." (Other Jews think this G-d business is a foolish conceit.)

When the Hebrew patriarch Jacob, with help from his conniving mother, Rebekah, fooled his blind father, Isaac, into blessing him instead of Jacob's brother, Esau, the words spoken accomplished a reality that Isaac believed he could not undo. We postmodern American Chris-

> The Hebrew tradition honors words by acknowledging their astonishing power.

tians, given a similar circumstance (which is hard enough to imagine), might well have said, were we Isaac and had we discovered the treachery, "Whoa, whoa. I take it back. Come here, Esau. You'll have the blessing, not your deceitful brother."

But that's because we don't understand the power of words in the same way that Jewish culture did then—and in many ways still does today. Words for many of us are cheap. Words may describe reality, or try to, but they can't change it much in the way that God's creative words did or in the way that Isaac's word of blessing on Jacob forever deprived Esau of what was rightfully his.[9]

People of faith would do well to recover some of that respect for the power and sacredness of words. Instead, we often are among those who spew out words as if from a fire hose, spraying them wantonly across the Internet via email, blogs, tweets, and whatnot. The supply of words today far exceeds the demand (which makes me wonder whether I should be writing this book). Worse, the supply of sacred words now gets simply overwhelmed by words that have no sacral value, no spirit of holiness, and that reflect no longing for eternal truths.

In stark contrast to our rush of words stands the one we Christians call the Word of God, Jesus. In him there is no bloat, no surfeit, no meaningless gushing of empty words. He speaks and the words shimmer with both the human and the divine. He simply is, and the Word glows with a love that will not let us go. Never mind that those determined folks in the Jesus Seminar have spent a lot of time voting with little colored beads about whether Jesus really said what he's reported to have said in this Gospel or that. That's a semi-interesting parlor game among people more interested in what they don't believe than in what they do. But their work does nothing to diminish or silence the eternal Word that Christ speaks to us, a Word of welcome, of compassion, of judgment, yes, but finally of acceptance and forgiveness—a word of faith.

> The supply of sacred words now gets simply overwhelmed by words that have no sacral value, no spirit of holiness.

Sometimes I am astonished and now and then even ashamed at how many words I have written in my career. One small measure of my apparently endless loquaciousness is that I have datelined out of more than 260 cities. This is my sixth book. I wrote a daily—weekdays, anyway—column for twenty-seven years. I have written a daily blog since December 2004, plus years' worth of regular columns for the *Presbyterian Outlook* and the *National Catholic Reporter*. And on and on.

Few of those words qualify as sacred. Many times they have been filler, stuffing, wadding, and bulk. Yet people of faith are called to think about the sacredness of words and to use words not to fill up or decorate otherwise-blessed silence but to make that silence sing of ceaseless meaning.

A monk friend offers me advice that I now offer to you: Speak. But only if it improves the silence.

LET'S TALK ABOUT THIS

What are the most sacred words you ever spoke or wrote? What made them so?

What words have spoken to you most powerfully, either for good or ill? Did you at the time consider them secular or sacred?

When you speak aloud, does it sometimes, always, or never improve the silence? Why?

Isn't water really thicker than blood?

Christianity is a bloody religion. I'm not referring to the millions of people over the centuries whom Christians have killed in the name of faith, though for sure there is that. (Indeed, Duke Divinity School theologian Stanley Hauerwas once told me that he has a sign on his office door from the Mennonite Central Committee responding to that history. It says: "A modest proposal for peace: Let the Christians of the world resolve not to kill one another.") Rather, I mean that in various ways blood is central to Christians' identity and to their destiny. And the idea of blood, not surprisingly, thus gets misused by some Christians who fear for their own destiny.

When I was a full-time columnist for the *Kansas City Star*, a man came to me and said he had a "burden" to minister to people in the media. Fine with me, I told him. We can use all the prayer and support we can get. So he started an organization called Media Fellowship that held occasional gatherings for newspaper reporters and others in the news media. But it soon became apparent that he was worried not about those of us at the paragraph factory or at radio and TV stations around town. Rather, he was worried about his own eternal fate.

"If I don't reach you and others in the media for Jesus Christ," he told me one day, "I will have your blood on my hands."

Well, I thought, soap and water should fix that. Then I thought that there are worse things to get on your hands than my blood, which drew on both German and Swedish heritage to become American, though it also spent part of my childhood in an officially diagnosed anemic state.

But his astonishingly self-centered vision of ministry managed to get true ministry completely backwards. Ministry means giving yourself away to others in need. It doesn't mean doing what you think is necessary to save your sorry ass from hell.

I never gave this man the satisfaction of hearing me say, "Jesus Christ is my personal Lord and Savior," words that he sought to drag out of me. And make no mistake: The precise and literal wording of such a confession was crucial for him to hear so he could feel that he had marked down another save on his ledger of the almost-damned. Instead, I tried to absolve him of worry about my eternal destiny and I began avoiding his phone calls and invitations to come to gatherings where, he said, the Holy Spirit would be present in a palpable way. I decided to let the Holy Spirit make the invitation directly to me and not have it come through this man. As a result, I was met with silence— beautiful, pregnant, holy silence.

Blood, of course, is a central image in Christianity. Drawing from ancient Hebrew sacrificial traditions, Christians often say that they are healed by Christ's blood, that the shedding of his blood—the perfect sacrifice of a perfect lamb—was necessary for us to be in a right relationship with God. Which is why hymns and rituals talk about being "washed in the blood of the Lamb." This focus on blood also produces some awkwardness, in that we Christians say Jesus was in the bloodline of King David, though, if so, that would have been through Joseph, who, in Christian theology, was not technically, not biologically, the father of Jesus. (Best to let that one go.)

> Ministry means giving yourself away to others in need. It doesn't mean doing what you think is necessary to save your sorry ass from hell.

I've long thought that this deep focus on blood was interesting but perhaps a bit off the mark, given that even Jesus thought it was off the mark. I'll explain. I once preached a sermon I called "Water Is Thicker Than Blood," in which I tried to make the point that the water of baptism creates an eternal family that is more lasting and more important than the family that blood creates. I used two stories from scripture to make my point. One was the story of Ruth, whose mother-in-law, Naomi, became, in effect, her family after the death of Ruth's husband, even though Ruth was a Moabite and Naomi was a Jew. The story includes this beautiful pledge from Ruth to Naomi: "Wherever you go, I will go; wherever you live, I will live. Your people will be my people, and your God will be my God. Wherever you die, I will die, and there I will be buried" (Ruth 1:16–17 NLT). It's a lovely commitment to family that is created by spirit and commitment, not by blood.

Similarly, I used the story from Mark 3 about Jesus's mother and brothers coming to see him, apparently to ask him to leave off this foolish preachy-healy stuff he was doing and come home:

> They stood outside and sent word for him to come out and talk with them. There was a crowd sitting around Jesus, and someone said, "Your mother and your brothers are outside asking for you." Jesus replied, "Who is my mother? Who are my brothers?" Then he looked around him and said, "Look, these are my mother and brothers. Anyone who does God's will is my brother and sister and mother." (Mark 3:31–35 NLT)

Jesus was not, I think, minimizing the importance of blood relations. After all, from the very cross he later asked John to take care of his mother. Rather, he was expanding the definition of family in the same way that the story of Ruth expanded it beyond blood.

So blood, like water, is an important image in Christian faith, but it's best to think of both blood and water as invitations to life, in that both of them make life possible and sustain it. I don't shy away from blood imagery, as some Christians do. I think blood imagery can help us understand the pain Jesus endured on the cross. But because faith is to be about life, I tend to move from thinking about the spilling of blood to thinking about the flowing of blood within each of us so that we may love God and love our neighbor. If blood didn't do that for us, I would lose faith in it.

It's best to think of both blood and water as invitations to life.

In My Blood

I carry with me,
like stigmata from ancestral wounds,
the injuries visited upon my parents,
my grandparents, and their own antecedents:

My almond-shaped eyes,
which children at boarding school in India
thought Asian—perhaps Chinese—
and derided as if having them were sinful.

My skittish heart,
unwilling to risk too much
or wander too far,
always afraid of being found foolish.

My blurred vision,
my arthritic joints,
my tendency toward
complex books and oily skin.

If this flawed bloodline is my desert,
I will walk in it,
seeking not revenge
but redemption.

LET'S TALK ABOUT THIS

Has anyone ever asked you to make a confession of faith? How did you respond? Is that how you'd respond today? Why?

Do you think the water of baptism creates a family more eternal than a family related by blood? Or is that just a theological word trick? Explain.

Is death just
an option?

In my book *Woodstock: A Story of Middle Americans*, I briefly describe the first encounter with death that I remember:

> When I was five years old or so, my mother plucked me
> from our front yard, where I was playing, and made me
> walk across the street with her to attend the in-home
> wake of a woman we called Grandma Moore—the first
> dead body I'd ever seen. I tried to get out of it by telling
> Mom I didn't want to go because I didn't want or need
> to see an old dead lady naked. (Why do dead people
> need clothes, after all? Good reasoning for a kid.) But
> Mom explained the tradition of dressing the dead to
> protect their dignity. And I went.[10]

After that, my experiences of death were several, and occasionally out of the ordinary. In India as a boy I was on the banks of the Ganges one day watching as a drowned student's body was hauled in—but only after a boat operator argued with the student's friends trying to save him about the price of helping. I attended the funeral of my paternal grandmother in 1953, when I was eight years old, and watched my maternal grandmother pat Grandma Tammeus's dead hands in the casket and wish her peace. Until then I didn't know it was all right to touch dead people in their caskets. I attended the funeral of a friend's mother who had committed suicide my freshman year in high school. She had asked that her body be left in our church sanctuary overnight, and it was. Also in my freshman year my paternal grandfather died, and I simply lost it when his casket was raised on an elevator-like device to be slid into a slot in a mausoleum. One night in college I was assigned by the newspaper for which I wrote to cover the murder of a man in a bar. When I got there the dead man was lying faceup on the floor, looking at all of us but not seeing any of us. Nearby the cash register said NO SALE. And all of this says nothing about the pets I watched die or the day my freakish two-foot-tall petunia plant collapsed and perished.

In Christian theological terms, death is the defeated enemy that doesn't know it's beaten, so it keeps on keeping on. Because it does, it paradoxically helps to give our life meaning. Even as I write this, for instance, I am thinking that I want to finish this book and see how readers react to it before death claims me. So I write with more purpose, more intensity. Death, among other circumstances, motivates me. It's hard to finish either writing or reading a book when you're dead. At least I think that's true. If I turn out to be wrong about that I'll try to let you know somehow.

What is also true—perhaps especially for people of faith—is that we will never understand our own lives if we don't understand our own deaths. And that is an increasingly difficult task because we live in a culture that seems to want nothing to do with death, a culture that, as I've already mentioned, seems to think that death is optional, that wants to hide away dead bodies the instant life slips out of them so no one has to see what really goes on next. As Caitlin Doughty writes in *Smoke Gets in Your Eyes: And Other Lessons from the Crematory*, "There has never been a time in the history of the world when a culture has broken so completely with traditional methods of body disposition and beliefs surrounding mortality."[11] (She's talking about us Americans.)

> In Christian theological terms, death is the defeated enemy that doesn't know it's beaten.

Understanding our own death ultimately means being at peace with the reality that we will cease to be—utterly.[12] If we are to move into an afterlife, that will be a gift of grace from God. Indeed, a core part of the Christian message is that God wants to be in eternal relationship with all of us, which is why the resurrection of Christ was so crucial (to use a small pun). It showed that God had defeated death and that one day, God would reconcile whatever needs to be reconciled, heal whatever needs to be healed, resurrect whatever needs resurrection, and, of course, love whoever needs love—and who doesn't?

> We will never understand our own lives if we don't understand our own deaths.

The thing about faith, however, is that it is not necessary to think about all this afterlife and resurrection stuff constantly. Once it's burned into your heart, you can simply get on with living a life of gratitude for it. That's really what genuine faith looks like—a life that says thank you, thank you, thank you. A well-known preacher once confided in me that he knows lots of people who think about heaven so much that they're no earthly good. In some ways I wish the Bible hadn't spent all the time it did talking about heaven and hell. It's been a huge distraction from living with the purpose of repairing the world, which is what my Jewish friends mean when they use the term *tikkun olam*.

I have spent a lot of time and ink writing about death over the years. In fact, the first chapter in my first book, *A Gift of Meaning*, is a column I wrote about my mother's own funeral in 1996.[13] Since then I've devoted lots of blog space and column inches to helping readers understand death. My own acquaintance with death has been helped in recent years by serving on the board of Kansas City Hospice & Palliative Care, a fabulous nonprofit organization that employs staff members who know how to make the final path as smooth as possible for dying people.[14]

But in all this, I confess that I have had trouble imagining not being. Yes, I can say that, in the end, I expect to be wrapped in the solicitous arms of a loving God. I even expect to be welcomed by Jesus. And I expect to be surprised (which maybe means it wouldn't be a surprise, but let that go). But somehow the state of not being alive on Earth is too much of a mystery for me. If you happen to be reading this after my death, let me know how my nonexistence feels. At the moment I just don't get it.

LET'S TALK ABOUT THIS

What was your first encounter with death? How has that continued to shape you, if at all?

Do you agree that America seems to be a death-denying culture? If so, why is that? If you agree that it shouldn't be, what can you do to change that?

Can we really have faith in a faithless age?

One of the inevitable consequences of the ways in which the Uncertainty Principle has pervaded nearly all of our thinking is that many people have embraced postmodernism without thinking carefully about its pluses and minuses, its ability to enlighten and its tendency to confuse and frustrate.

Which is to say that more and more people have been willing to move away from religious traditions without replacing them with much of value. Recent polls suggest that nearly 23 percent of the American adult population now identifies as religiously unaffiliated.[15] That is quite different from not believing in God. Polls consistently show that more than 90 percent of the American population claims a belief in God, which continues to make the United States one of the most religiously developed nations in the world. But the movement toward no affiliation suggests that fewer and fewer people buy into the metanarratives that historically have helped to shape our nation.

Metanarratives, or the "big stories" that are overarching and help to define the smaller stories of our culture, once were pervasive. Although not unquestioned, they certainly were widely accepted, and it's their rejection that defines postmodernism. You can name some of them as easily as I can:

- America is a city set on a hill to give light to the nations—in effect, deputized by God.

- We are a light of liberty for the world.
- Anyone can grow up to be president.
- You can pull yourself up by your own bootstraps.
- Ben Franklin's twin idols, industriousness and frugality, will take you far in life.
- In a world of darkness and evil, we Americans—especially those of us inside the white, Anglo-Saxon tradition[16]—represent goodness and morality, for God has shed his grace on us.

These and many other similar metanarratives have in large part been tossed on history's trash heap. Oh, it's not that they don't still contain some truth and it's not that they don't still have many followers. Rather, it's that most of us know by now so many exceptions to the pictures they paint that they seem simplistic and misleading. They were for a more innocent time that often mistook myth, allegory, and metaphor for literal historical truth.

> We are becoming an increasingly unanchored (some would say freer) culture, one that can't point to a cohesive story that somehow embraces all of us and gives us meaning.

Without these and similar metanarratives and without the social or religious affiliations that constantly remind us of something larger than ourselves, we are becoming an increasingly unanchored (some would say freer) culture, one that can't point to a cohesive story that somehow embraces all of us and gives us meaning. What today, after all, is the "American Dream"? At times we seem to be set adrift in a sea of meaninglessness that threatens to move us toward what Albert Camus said in *The Myth of Sisyphus* was the only "really serious philosophical question, and that is suicide."

In the face of such bleakness, what possible word can faith speak, especially Christian faith, which itself has been scattered and shattered into millions of pieces and is, therefore, a house divided?

The answer may be surprising both to Christians whose faith has become rather rote, dormant, and unexamined, and to non-Christians who don't grasp what Christianity really teaches about the nature of the Godhead. The answer is: the living Christ.

The word that Christianity wants to speak to the world is the Word itself, a resurrected, living, vibrant, generative being who is seeking out the lost and lonely; the sad and dispirited; the anxious and hopeless; the needy, unprepared, and fearful. It's not that Jesus was resurrected two thousand years ago and then slipped into heaven to attend an endless round of celebratory parties for a job well done. Rather, it's that the spirit of the living Christ has been set loose in the world today and wants to transform lives. No matter what it sounds like at first, this is not woo-woo stuff, not crazy talk about some bouncy spirit that you can access only with the right kind of mantra or spiritual discipline.

> The spirit of the living Christ has been set loose in the world today and wants to transform lives. No matter what it sounds like at first, this is not woo-woo stuff, not crazy talk.

Here's one way to think about this: In the midst of murder and rape, war and robbery, white-collar crime and abuse of children—in other words, in light of what we know about ourselves as human beings— how do we explain all the goodness in the world? How do we account for all the volunteers who give of themselves to people to need? What are we to make of all the people who give to charity, rescue the homeless, feed the hungry, comfort the abused—often with no hope of being repaid? When disaster strikes, what motivates people—whether Christian or not—to respond with money, talent, time, prayer, presence, and tears?

A Christian answer is this: When you see such things, you are seeing the spirit of the living God, which is to say Christ, at work. Our task is to identify where God in Christ is busy in the world and find ways to connect, to volunteer, and even to point to the goodness and give God the credit.

It may seem both odd and ridiculous to search for the living, moving Christ in the midst of decay, woundedness, chaos, disaster, death.

But that is exactly where we should expect to find him. The great modern theologian Jürgen Moltmann, whom I once had the privilege of hearing speak, got it right in his book *The Crucified God* when he wrote that all modern theology must be created "in earshot of the dying cry of Jesus."[17] If theology cannot offer some way forward from suffering, evil, death, and destruction, if it can't whisper a word of hope in a time of abandonment, if it has nothing to say to a mother grieving the death of her daughter (such as, "God was the first to shed tears over this"), to a child crying out for a dead parent, to a coastal community flattened by a hurricane, then it has nothing worth saying at all—even if what it does say fails to answer every question and is, therefore, not completely satisfying.

Faith is not about believing this doctrine or that confession of faith. It's not about saying yes to a particular tradition's way of explaining how and why the world was created or how and why some day it might all come to an end. Faith, rather, is simply the desire of the human spirit and the human soul to be in harmony with the divine, to feel at home in the creation, to be convinced that there is so much we cannot know that what we think we do know may, in fact, be wrong. Faith is the commitment to live forward, to live in hope and joy and laughter and surprise anyway. Anyway.

Faith, frankly, is irrational, in part because it's a gift, which is one reason it makes so much sense and is so beautiful.

LET'S TALK ABOUT THIS

Which of the metanarratives mentioned in this chapter still hold at least some truth for you and which have you abandoned as meaningless? Why?

With all the suffering and evil in the world, how do you personally explain the presence of so much goodness?

What is your own calling?

In my branch of Christianity, the Reformed Tradition, there's a strong emphasis on being "called" to a particular way of life, to a particular form of ministry, to a special vocation meant for you. Indeed, the word "vocation" itself is derived from the Latin word *vocare*, which means to call. (For you young readers, calling is what we did with phones before we could text.)

This idea of calling in a vocational and spiritual sense is tied into the biblical notion that each of us has been given certain gifts, whether it's the ability to write well, speak well, do algebra well, or shoot a basketball like no one else. (Did you know that the Holy Spirit cares about basketball? Well, *I* certainly have cared about it and I am glad I was gifted with a dependable sixteen-foot jump shot, which I still could make if I could find anyone my age still willing to play.)

In 1 Corinthians, the Apostle Paul talks in some detail about such gifts, which he says come from the Holy Spirit. He says, "A spiritual gift is given to each of us so we can help each other. To one person the Spirit gives the ability to give wise advice; to another the same Spirit gives a message of special knowledge. The same Spirit gives great faith to another, and to someone else the one Spirit gives the gift of healing" (12:7–9 NLT). And on it goes.

Paul's immediate concern was the fledgling Jesus Movement of his day, which eventually morphed into Christianity after its reluctant parting from Judaism, to use the phrase religious studies scholar Julie Galambush took as the title of her book *The Reluctant Parting: How the New Testament's Jewish Writers Created a Christian Book.*[18] Paul wanted people in the newly forming movement to rely on one another, to work together as a team, not to worry individually about needing to fill all the roles that were being called for in this new movement within first-century Judaism (which really should be listed as first-century Judaisms—plural—given the variety of movements within that tradition then).

It's a little harder in twenty-first-century America to make sense of the idea of "call." For one thing, it's not uncommon that over the course of a working lifetime people today will change not just jobs but whole career paths half a dozen or more times. My career was a little unusual in that after college I had only two full-time newspaper jobs—one that lasted a bit more than three years and one that, full time, lasted more than thirty-six years. I truly felt called to be a writer. I learned early on that almost no one makes a living as a poet so I went into the more turbulent business of writing news and opinion. I often told people that I would have been a writer even if my career had been putting fenders on Fords. The truth is that I must write. I don't know what I think about things until I write about them. I can't find my way through life save through doing the task Annie Dillard describes in *The Writing Life*:

> This idea of calling in a vocational and spiritual sense is tied into the biblical notion that each of us has been given certain gifts.

> When you write, you lay out a line of words. The line of words is a miner's pick, a wood-carver's gouge, a surgeon's probe. You wield it, and it digs a path you follow. Soon you find yourself deep in new territory. Is it a dead end, or have you located the real subject? You will know tomorrow, or this time next year.[19]

Once we discover our gifts, we are obliged to nourish them, bring them to full flower, figure out what good they might do for humanity. There is almost nothing as sad as someone with a true gift for some task or art who has failed to develop it and use it.

Some people, of course, have many gifts and ultimately must choose one on which to focus. I recall sitting down with my youngest stepson when he was in high school and asking him to make a list of the things he thought he was good at and that might be a career choice. He wrote and wrote and when he was done he had made note of more than a dozen possibilities—each one of which he seemed to be gifted in. It was quite an impressive list. Now some twenty-plus years later, he has made educational and career choices that have narrowed those options considerably. Some day he may move off his current path in the business world and see where his musical and artistic talents can take him. The point is, of course, to recognize what the gifts are and to nurture them until they become, in effect, a ministry.

> There is almost nothing as sad as someone with a true gift for some task or art who has failed to develop it and use it.

Faith helps us identify our gifts. Faith encourages us not to waste them. Faith is the force that helps us see our gifts as possibilities for ministry, which means nothing more and nothing less than giving ourselves away to others in need. I am called to write. Do I sometimes worry that I am the one doing the calling? Of course. Can I be certain that God wants me to be a writer? No, not certain. But faith is what gives me consistent clues that I'm on the right path—clues that show me that my writing is making at least some difference for good, offering wisdom and insight in a world desperate for those qualities. In other words, if I were using my writing to create operations manuals for al-Qaida operatives, I hope I would sense that I was not just wasting my talent but also using it to create destructive trash. The fact that there are writers who do create operations manuals for al-Qaida operatives causes me considerable pain, but also makes me wonder how the hell their faith has led them to such dark duty. Faith is supposed to be better than that. Perhaps what led them down this foreboding trail was all the unquestioned answers they have.

LET'S TALK ABOUT THIS

Have you ever sensed a vocational or life path calling that you believed was of divine origin? What made you feel confident you were right about that?

If you were asked to identify your spiritual gifts, what would they be? Are you using them? If so, how?

What can we learn from the Celts?

To say a word about the influence Celtic spirituality has had on me—and can have on you—I want to return to the story I told at the start of this book.

As I wrote there, I watched the sunrise in the Himalayas on Easter Sunday 1956, and discovered in that God-filled moment an attachment to the concept and reality of resurrection, of redemption.

Much later, as I became better acquainted with Celtic spirituality, mostly through the writings of—and conversations with—my friend John Philip Newell, former warden of Iona Abbey in Scotland, I recognized that my sunrise experience was in deep harmony with the Celtic idea that God's spirit is in all and that the place to look for God is in the ordinary, everyday world.[20]

In Philip's book *Listening for the Heartbeat of God: A Celtic Spirituality*, he quotes the ancient (and often wrongly discredited, Philip argues) British monk Pelagius on this subject:

> "Look at the animals roaming the forest: God's spirit dwells within them. Look at the birds flying across the sky: God's spirit dwells within them. Look at the tiny insects crawling in the grass: God's spirit dwells within them. Look at the fish in the river and sea: God's spirit dwells within them. There is no creature on earth in whom God is absent."[21]

This is not pantheism, which proffers the idea that because God is in everything, everything is therefore God and God *is* all things. Rather,

Praise to God, the great Creator,
Praise to God, incarnate Son,
Praise to God, the Holy Spirit,
Praise to God, the three in one.
Yet beyond all words and titles—
Sovereign, Spirit, Perfect Lamb—
Lives a truth that leaves us silent:
God is still the great I Am.

LET'S TALK ABOUT THIS

If you're a Christian, does it matter to you whether you have a way of explaining the Trinity that makes sense or is that just a meaningless theological enigma? Explain your thoughts.

Has anyone from a faith tradition different from yours ever asked you to explain the Trinity? What did you say? Did it enlighten or confuse the other person?

How did Christians get race and other matters so wrong?

At the 2015 National Prayer Breakfast, President Barack Obama gave a well-reasoned talk about some things that are right with religion and some things that, over centuries of history, have gone wrong with it. It was, in certain ways, sort of standard-issue prayer breakfast material, but as soon as he mentioned that Christians across history have committed or supported some terrible deeds and policies, from the Crusades to slavery to Jim Crow, there was a quick backlash from a lot of people, many of whom would identify themselves as conservative (politically and religiously).

The reaction was both loud and ludicrous, which sometimes is what you get as a response when you speak the truth. As background, here are a few key remarks from the president:

> As we speak, around the world, we see faith inspiring people to lift up one another—to feed the hungry and care for the poor, and comfort the afflicted and make peace where there is strife.... We see faith driving us to do right.
>
> But we also see faith being twisted and distorted, used as a wedge—or, worse, sometimes used as a weapon. From a school in Pakistan to the streets of Paris, we have seen violence and terror perpetrated by those who profess to stand up for faith, their faith, professed

to stand up for Islam, but, in fact, are betraying it. We see ISIL, a brutal, vicious death cult that, in the name of religion, carries out unspeakable acts of barbarism—terrorizing religious minorities like the Yezidis, subjecting women to rape as a weapon of war, and claiming the mantle of religious authority for such actions....

Humanity has been grappling with these questions throughout human history. And lest we get on our high horse and think this is unique to some other place, remember that during the Crusades and the Inquisition, people committed terrible deeds in the name of Christ. In our home country, slavery and Jim Crow all too often was justified in the name of Christ.[27]

As I say, these on-target remarks unleashed a firestorm of criticism, most of it from people imagining that the president was saying that the ISIS (or ISIL) terrorists are somehow the moral equivalent of Christians today. Which, of course, is not what he said at all.

A small sample of the arrows slung at Obama:

- "Hey, American Christians—Obama just threw you under the bus in order to defend Islam."
  —radio talk show shock jock Michael Graham[28]

- The president's comments were "dangerously irresponsible."
  —Rep. Marlin Stutzman, a Republican from Indiana[29]

- "Obama's ignorance is astounding and his comparison is pernicious."
  —Bill Donohue of the Catholic League[30]

- "Today's remarks by the president were inappropriate and his choice of venue was insulting to every person of faith at a time when Christians are being crucified, beheaded, and persecuted across the Middle East."
  —former Senator Rick Santorum,
    a Pennsylvania Republican[31]

What, if anything, does all this have to do with faith as I'm trying to describe it in this book? It has to do directly with faith because faith that does not know or cannot understand its own history operates in the dark. Faith that denies the rocky road its tradition has traversed is lost. Faith that does not have the courage to acknowledge its imperfections is delusional and, in the end, cannot be sustained. Faith that cannot repent of its past or thinks there's nothing in its past that requires repentance is not to be trusted.[32]

I certainly am not saying that twenty-first-century Christians should feel personal guilt for the Crusades, the Spanish Inquisition, or slavery. Our spiritual ancestors made the choices to support those movements or institutions—we didn't. But this history is part of our larger story. The very faith that Christians profess today was stained and dishonored in the past by actions and policies that previous Christians chose. To ignore that or pretend it didn't happen would be like imagining that all the early American settlers and pioneers always treated Native Americans with respect and love. For history to be useful in understanding today's context, it must be told in all its glory but also in all its anguish and errors.

One of the dangers of failing to do that is that we will imagine that when we pledge allegiance to our faith we are part of a long and unblemished history of goodness and light. This not only relieves us of responsibility for correcting what our ancestors got wrong, it also leaves us imagining that the path forward will be smooth and without difficult moral choices. That would be an unguided journey into disaster.

Faith requires clear eyes, despite the assertion in 2 Corinthians 5:7 that "We live by faith and not by sight" (CEB). Those words are not suggesting that we don't need to have our antennae tuned to what's past, present, and future. Rather, they are an acknowledgment that we cannot be certain of what is to come and that we live by metaphor, allegory, and myth. The purpose of historical honesty is not to beat ourselves up over what those who preceded us did. Rather, it's to keep from making similarly terrible choices and to know that we are fallible and in need of salvation both in this life and in the one to come.

Faith that walks with historical blinders on will almost certainly miss the generative, life-giving movement of the Holy Spirit, the God of possibilities, the God whom we are to notice so we can be open to yielding to the path we're being shown. The truth about history liberates us to live out a faith that can help make the rough places smooth, the paths straight, the valleys filled, and the mountains leveled so that all will see the salvation God offers.

LET'S TALK ABOUT THIS

How much of the history of your own faith tradition, if any, do you know well enough to describe with reasonable accuracy to someone unfamiliar with it?

What in the historical record of your religion makes you most proud and what makes you most ashamed? Why?

FAITH IN LIGHT OF DOUBT

Must scripture be historically accurate to be true?

The opening words of Genesis, as the novelist Kurt Vonnegut once noted, are clear, simple, and "well within the writing skills of a lively fourteen-year-old: 'In the beginning, God created the heavens and the earth.'"[1]

They are so simple that it took me a long time to realize that when I say, as I did in the previous sentence, that the words are clear, I'm lying.

If the words were clear, why would I have these questions about just that one sentence?

- When was the beginning?
- Who is this God you mention?
- How did God create whatever God created?
- Heavens? There's more than one heaven?
- Would Earth, as it looks today, be anything like what it looked like at the moment of creation? Or did creation take a lot longer than a moment?

Whoever wrote those words in Genesis—and, despite the traditional claim, I'm pretty sure it wasn't Moses—didn't seem worried about anticipating bothersome questions before they get asked.

When I was in confirmation class in 1958 at First Presbyterian Church of Woodstock, our pastor, the Reverend Cecil C. Urch, dealt with the two Genesis creation stories by talking with us confirmands about geologic eras—you know, Paleozoic, Mesozoic, and Cenozoic, like that. I suspected even back then that this was his way of suggesting to us that a literal interpretation of the Bible would lead us astray, as it will.

Much later in my life, Don Fisher, then an associate pastor at my church in Kansas City, used to guide us in that same way with this phrase about something we'd read in scripture: "I don't know if that's factual or historically accurate, but I believe it's true."

The problem, however, with giving people permission to recognize that the Bible has to be interpreted to be understood and, therefore, often cannot be read as literal history, is that this requires some level of interpretive freedom on the part of people who frequently would prefer simply to be told what something means. They want scripture to be black or white, not gray.[2] Freedom of interpretation does not, of course, mean that all interpretations are valid or of equal value. Instead, there must be—and are—necessary rules for exegesis. Without them, anything goes. But once people realize that it's possible to have a good-faith interpretation that differs from someone else's good-faith interpretation, life becomes so complicated that lots of people simply abandon the interpretive ship in favor of bromides: "The Bible says it, I believe it, that settles it." Taken as an undivided trinity of meaning, those are three of the most sacrilegious statements that it's possible for a Christian or a Jew to make.

> Preference for bumper-sticker biblical analysis is one reason a mid-2012 Gallup poll showed that nearly half of Americans believe that the Earth was created all at once about ten thousand years ago.

Perhaps this preference for bumper-sticker biblical analysis is one reason a mid-2012 Gallup poll showed that nearly half of Americans believe that the Earth was created all at once about ten thousand years ago.[3] That's a pinchbeck position that can be arrived at only after irresponsibly abandoning one's obligation to read the Bible critically (and lovingly) and to read it with a foundational notion of what metaphor, myth, and allegory are all about. If we read the Bible critically, we are not saying that the words in it aren't sacred or divinely inspired, that they're not, in some sense, the Word of God or that they are merely a secular collection of ancient writings. Rather, reading the Bible critically means that the reader has decided to take the Bible seriously. For the reality is that you can take the Bible seriously or you can take it literally but you can't do both, although even that acknowledgment does not mean that there is no actual history in the Bible. What biblical literalists have done, among other misguided deeds, is to throw out the spirit of the ancient Jewish practice of *midrash*, which is a way of inter-

> You can take the Bible seriously or you can take it literally but you can't do both.

preting holy writ that allows for multiple interpretations, not just one authoritative understanding of what was written. Those who use *midrash* are obliged to acknowledge that their own understanding of scripture may be wrong and certainly is never the final interpretation.

The remarkable thing about this collection of books called the Bible is that it still speaks to us today about eternal meaning. It's not a rules book, a guide book that you can simply open to find immediate answers to questions about whether to put your mother in a nursing home or whether to donate part of your IRA to charity for a tax deduction. Rather, it is the story of a people to whom Christians and Jews (to say nothing of Muslims) today still have a direct connection. And thus, in many ways, it is the prelude to our own personal stories.

And speaking of stories, it helps to remember that almost every culture has its own creation story. I was in Vancouver, British Columbia, a few years ago and visited the University of British Columbia's Museum of Anthropology. There I saw artist Bill Reid's amazing "Raven and the First Men" sculpture, depicting the Haida creation myth, a complicated, fascinating story of how things came to be.[4] It is just one of countless myths about the origin of the world. What matters, in the end, is not so much which creation story is historically accurate (good luck with that) but which one gives us a sense of purpose, a sense of meaning, a context that allows life to matter.

For my life, I have chosen the creation stories in Genesis—not because they are factual or historically accurate but because they speak truth about how we got to here and how and why we got to now.

To Get to Now

To get to now,
with all its regrets, its losses, its hopes,
we have traveled past exploding stars,
full of tiny pieces
of who we are
so that now
there is something in us
older than ourselves.
And past the birth
of our very sun,
whose crazy sprays of flame
lick and spit at space with so much fury
that it cannot—will not—last forever.
And past the first cells,
having sex in the only sexless way
they knew how.
Past the early nervous systems
of jellyfish, who must have had
awesome reasons to be nervous.
Past the first fish with the first bones,
and the first sea animals to leave this
forwarding address as home: land.
Past the first insects and trees,
dinosaurs and flowers,
and past, finally, mammals,
who would include, eventually,
the image of God,
though of course God's image
was also baked into all the rest.

We have come to now
past the first fire, the first house,
the first warrior's breastplate,
past the first crops planted on purpose,
the first kings and queens,
and flying machines,
and the first bomb to fall from the latter
on orders from one of the former.
We did not get to now
starting from yesterday or last week
or from the day our grandparents
married and made love.
No, getting to now
has been a long, jagged,
amazing, unpredictable,
enervating journey.
No wonder that some days
it feels as if we have
carried the world
to this time and place.
Carried the world.
That is exactly what we've done
to get to now.

LET'S TALK ABOUT THIS

What is your most troubling question about what you read
in the Bible—and what parts of the Bible give you the most
comfort? Why?

On whom do you rely when you have questions about how to
interpret the Bible? What are the books you turn to for this task?
Why?

Can we recover if we tumble off the path?

When I was in high school, trying to imagine what life might be about, a teacher assigned us to read *Of Human Bondage* by W. Somerset Maugham. Here is a brief section that jackhammered into my heart and led me astray for several years:

> Thinking of Cronshaw, Philip remembered the Persian rug which he had given him, telling him that it offered an answer to his question upon the meaning of life; and suddenly the answer occurred to him: he chuckled: now that he had it, it was like one of the puzzles which you worry over till you are shown the solution and then cannot imagine how it could ever have escaped you. The answer was obvious. Life had no meaning. On the earth, satellite of a star speeding through space, living things had arisen under the influence of conditions which were part of the planet's history; and as there had been a beginning of life upon it so, under the influence of other conditions, there would be an end: man, no more significant than other forms of life, had come not as the climax of creation but as a physical reaction to the environment.[5]

The flaccid and facile theology contained in this passage stood against almost everything I had been taught as a member of a Christian church. Yet some strange light went off in my head the minute I read it and I threw over what my elders and other teachers had given me. Here, I thought, finally, was truth. Here was fearless science that needed only itself to explain the cosmos, including the very question that science, I now know, can never answer: purpose. Perhaps the attractiveness of this approach to a teenager was that it freed me from the moral obligation to understand that I had moral obligations.

When, years later, I revisited the passage to see what I had misunderstood, I was stunned by how unprepared I seemed to have been as a teen to encounter—and, when necessary, counter—such thinking. By the time a person reaches high school (or surely within one's high school years), he or she should have been exposed to critical-thinking techniques, the process of comparing and contrasting, of verifying and finding in the argument examples of unsupported assumptions, propaganda, and incogitant bilge.

In retrospect, as I've already hinted, I put at least a bit of the blame on the leaders of my church, who apparently didn't encourage enough conversation about life's stubborn questions or who couldn't find ways to make me listen seriously. It takes discernment to know when a young person is ready to start engaging the mysteries of theodicy, the processes of myth, metaphor, and allegory, even the difference between doctrine and truth. In Christianity, after all, truth is not a doctrine or a dogma. Truth, instead, is a person, Christ Jesus. And although certain formulations of doctrine can point toward truth, can illuminate some of the meaning of truth, can open us up to receiving truth, they are not the same as truth.

Perhaps I'm being a little hard on my Sunday school teachers, parents, and others. Even in the allegedly bucolic 1950s and early '60s, it was hard to find time to engage impressionable teenagers in profound dialogue about the meaning of life, about the eternal questions. And it's only gotten worse since then.

> It takes discernment to know when a young person is ready to start engaging the mysteries of theodicy, the processes of myth, metaphor, and allegory.

> In Christianity, after all, truth is not a doctrine or a dogma. Truth, instead, is a person, Christ Jesus.

I'm not suggesting that we discourage young people from their doubts, their spiky questions. In the long run it may well be impossible to own faith without having journeyed through the valley of the shadow of doubt or without having asked disconcerting questions or without pretending that we know much more than we do. But what a blessing it would be if all young people had mentors, teachers, parents, grandparents, friends who would serve as guides, chaperones, escorts through the thicket of questions that must be raised in each generation.

With such people we might avoid what the eighteenth-century French philosopher Denis Diderot said he encountered: "I have only a small flickering light to guide me in the darkness of a thick forest. Up comes a theologian and blows it out."[6]

THE PLAN

My eyes followed the small green lizard
in her twitched bobbing and weaving,
her nomadic life of desert pirouettes
beneath the broom baccharis
and the stick-figure shadows
of the cane cholla.

The yellowish stripes on her back
in quiver-dance motion
created the kind of TV screen pattern
I used to see on our Stromberg-Carlson
in the 1950s before Milton Berle
would come on in a dress.

In five seconds, she moved
north, northeast, west, southeast,
northwest, east, south, and finally north again
before she stopped,

simply stopped in the snakeweed
and waited for her plan.

I am that lizard,
moving aerobically through
the snakeweed of my life,
using up compass points
as if the supply of them
were limitless.

Only I'm hiding now
under a big sagebrush,
wondering where my plan is,
wondering if maybe this lizard
knows that pure motion
is the only plan that works.

LET'S TALK ABOUT THIS

When did you most go astray in life? How did you find your way back, if you did?

What were you once sure of that a theologian or a pastor or another person of faith later made you doubt? Where are you with that issue today? What did you once doubt that you're now pretty sure of?

Are we saved by faith or works?

There is a tendency in Protestantism—a tendency that sometimes entraps me—to think that the last word about faith is grace, and that once it's uttered there is nothing more to say. The Apostle Paul probably is to blame for this. He, after all, is the one who wrote in the second chapter of Ephesians: "For it is by grace you have been saved, through faith—and this is not from yourselves, it is the gift of God—not by works, so that no one can boast" (2:8–9 NIV).

Paul is exactly right about that, of course, but often the response from people is that this means they need to do nothing in response to the pure, unmerited favor that grace is. Thus they fall into the trap that, as I've already mentioned, Dietrich Bonhoeffer identified as "cheap grace." For that reason, I want to say a word on behalf of good works.

When my mother died in 1996, I spoke at her funeral and quoted from the New Testament book of James, which Martin Luther, founder of the Protestant Reformation, dismissed as "an epistle of straw" (he later changed his mind) because he thought it promoted not grace but what we now call "works righteousness," the idea that we can earn our way into heaven. I quoted from the second chapter of James to indicate that Mom sought to live by this admonition: "... faith by itself isn't enough. Unless it produces good deeds, it is dead and useless" (2:17 NLT).

> Once healthy faith is in us, it metabolizes as a life of gratitude.

Once healthy faith is in us, it metabolizes as a life of gratitude. Gratitude is demonstrated by the way we treat others, respond to the needs of people around us, seek to comfort the aggrieved, soothe the brokenhearted, bind up the wounded, repair the world. All of this work of mercy, compassion, and love gets us no eternal reward at all. In fact, an eternal reward is not why we do it. We do it because we want to show gratitude to God for what God already has done for us. We do it because we know we are called to love and care for others. We do it because it's just the right thing to do and we need not have long, philosophical arguments about something so obvious. (And we also do it for a reward because, to face the sorry truth about ourselves, our motives are always mixed. Sigh.)

> Works righteousness puts the cart before the horse. Faith, by contrast, puts the heart before the course.

Even the remarkable Benjamin Franklin, a quasi-deist, understood all of this when he wrote,

> I think vital religion has always suffered when ortho-
> doxy is more regarded than virtue. And the Scripture
> assures me that at the last day we shall not be examined
> by what we *thought*, but what we *did* ... that we did good
> to our fellow creatures.[7]

Of course, too much of this kind of thinking also leads us astray. It draws us into the thought that all that's required for salvation, in an eternal sense, is to "be a good person," as the phrase so often goes. Never mind that Jesus himself asked not to be called "good" because only God is good. And never mind that the idea of being a good person as a prerequisite for getting into heaven translates into what I've already mentioned, "works righteousness." Works righteousness gets it all back-ward. We don't do good works to please God, we do good works to say thanks to God for God's love and mercy toward us, expressed in all kinds of ways, including through the life, ministry, death, and resurrection of

Jesus Christ. Works righteousness puts the cart before the horse. Faith, by contrast, puts the heart before the course.

Yet it is hard not to imagine that somehow God is more pleased with us if we visit the prisoner, feed the hungry, clothe the naked, and house the homeless than if we do none of those deeds or, worse, commit acts that destroy instead of acts that build up. It is in that sense that good works, while not sufficient to merit an eternal relationship with God, are nonetheless evidence that our faith is rooted in the proper place and is in harmony with the life Jesus urged his followers to live.

Faith without good works may be dead, but good works without faith are rootless, hollow—and yet much to be preferred to evil works, whether motivated by religion or by something else. So I praise good works and ask that you grant me the grace to get away with it in this instance.

LET'S TALK ABOUT THIS

Have you ever believed that your good works will be enough to get you into heaven? Do you believe that today? Why?

What does living a life of gratitude look like? Whom do you know who best exemplifies such a life?

What can we do when Radio God goes off the air?

Here's a small secret that people of faith are reluctant to admit: We sometimes feel that God has abandoned us. It may be a momentary thing or, more often, the divine silence can last a terribly long time, even as long as most of a lifetime. (Even Mother Teresa experienced this. You can read about her estrangement from God in *Mother Teresa: Come Be My Light*.[8]) Feeling abandoned by God eventually happens to everyone who makes some kind of commitment to faith.

What lots of us don't understand, however, is that we simply must experience this sense of abandonment for there to be any possibility that we'll have real and meaningful hope—hope that, as the late French Reformed theologian Jacques Ellul says, "is indeed that which most completely expresses the will of this God."[9] Like an alcoholic, we must hit bottom, run out of resources, conclude that God has left us for dead before there is any chance of recovery.

Perhaps more clearly than any other theologian or writer I know, Ellul understood the relationship between our inevitable experience of feeling abandoned and the hope we so desperately seek. Hope, he writes (in the gender-exclusive language typical of the 1970s), "is man's answer to God's silence."[10]

Ellul simply assumes that we all will experience God's silence. And, of course, we will. Part of it may be God's decision not to speak to us through the various means God has available to do so. But I suspect that a larger part of what we call God's silence has to do with our thick-headed inability or unwillingness to pay attention, our failure to notice the many ways in which God seeks to get our attention, whether that's through sacred writ, the presence of others, the glories of nature, or some unlikely event that we chalk up as mere coincidence. This inattention is what the poet Christian Wiman calls "the self willfully held apart from God."[11]

> Part of what we call God's silence has to do with our thick-headed inability or unwillingness to pay attention.

Whatever the cause, the sense that God has abandoned us can be extraordinarily painful, as we know not only from our own lives but also from reading the story of Jesus's crucifixion, when, quoting Psalm 22, he cries out to ask why God has deserted him. The feeling of being alone in the universe can cause physical pain and bring us to our knees emotionally—to our knees in surrender and to our knees in a prayerful plea for relief.

Only then can the idea of hope mean much of anything. As Ellul puts it:

> Hope comes alive in the dreary silence of God, in our loneliness before a closed heaven, in our abandonment. God is silent, so it's man who is going to speak. But he is not going to speak in God's place, nor in order to decorate the silence, nor in taking his own word for a Word from God. Man is going to express his hope that God's silence is neither basic nor final, nor a cancellation of what we had laid hold of as a Word from God.[12]

When we have felt Radio God go silent, off the air—as I did in the years leading up to my divorce and as I did when the 9/11 terrorists murdered my nephew—and thus when we most acutely feel abandoned, like Job, we simply must protest. We must speak of this aloud to confirm the reality but also to urge God to be God, to insist that God keep promises. Ellul calls this "a challenge directed at God. Hence, in some sense, it could be said that hope is blasphemous. It actually rejects the decision of God's silence."[13] Beyond that, it's biblical. You can find it, for instance, on full display in these words from verses 13 and 14 of Psalm 88: "But I cry to you for help, Lord; in the morning my prayer comes before you. Why, Lord, do you reject me and hide your face from me?" (NIV). The psalmist's cry echoes much of the book of Job. And you should know that Job in no way was a patient man.

This challenge, this rejection of God's silence, this insistence that God show up and be God is, of course, exactly what God wants from us. (And it's what, in general, Jews are much better at than Christians, in my experience.) It is a sign that, finally, we take God seriously, that we trust God's promises, believe in God's presence, power, and possibilities. In a time of abandonment, our screams into the abyss are not signs of weakness or insanity. They are, rather, signs that we now are able to have hope in God. This is the kind of hope that is not just unnecessary when God is speaking clearly to us, when we feel God's overwhelming presence and light but perhaps even impossible to experience. But when the divine light grows dim or goes out, our response must be this confrontational, demanding, indefatigable hope.

> In a time of abandonment, our screams into the abyss are not signs of weakness or insanity. They are, rather, signs that we now are able to have hope in God.

Faith understands the difference between this kind of in-the-trenches hope and the silly and trivial hope the world often tries to peddle to us—hope that hangs its hat on squishy poetry and amateur rainbows painted on syrupy greeting cards. Genuine faith will cast its lot with the former—this high-cost, demanding, determined hope—every time.

Call it blasphemous if you want to, but I think God is most in love with us, most proud of us when—in the face of what Ellul called a "closed heaven"—we shout out in anger, "God, you unreliable bastard, show up. Now." Though probably it wouldn't hurt to add a "please."

LET'S TALK ABOUT THIS

What's the longest you've gone feeling estranged from or abandoned by God? How did the estrangement end, if it ever did?

How do you define hope in a religious sense? Is it merely optimism? Or is it something deeper? And if it's deeper, how do you explain the difference between hope and optimism?

Is the kingdom
of heaven for
now or later?

Perhaps it would be helpful to say more about the living Christ, given that his birth, life, death, and resurrection are at the very heart of Christianity. But there's no sense writing one more biographical sketch of Jesus of Nazareth (almost an impossibility) or either outlining or deconstructing traditional Christology in some systematic form. All that's been done. And done. And done.

Rather, let's think briefly about what any of that has to do with how we live and, thus, with faith.

We have a choice. We can focus on the Apostle Paul's emphasis on the work of salvation that Christ did on Earth. As Paul wrote in 1 Corinthians 15:14, "and if Christ has not been raised, then our proclamation has been in vain, and your faith has been in vain" (NRSV). The idea of eternal salvation due to and through the resurrection is what many people today mean when they use the term "gospel." And it's also part of traditional church teaching. But while I'm not ignoring or dismissing that, the captivating alternative is to focus on what Jesus himself meant by the gospel, or good news. In Matthew 4:17, Jesus says: "Change your hearts and lives! Here comes the kingdom of heaven!" (CEB).

For Jesus, as I've said, the good news was that transformation is available now—right in the midst of this hostile empire. You can live in the reign of God today. You can cast off the stultifying, self-aggrandizing, ungenerous ways that the world encourages us to live and, instead, show compassion, mercy, justice, and love. Will doing all that get us to heaven? Yes, if by "heaven" you mean living as if God were real and alive and present and interested in our individual lives now. No, if by "heaven" you mean some postdeath destination where we learn how to play the harp and sing all day, for if there is such a place, your good works, your compassion, mercy, justice, and love won't earn you a spot there. If there is such a place, only God's grace will grant you entrance. (And, yes, the church historically has affirmed that there is such a place or, at any rate, such a state of being. And I affirm the church's teaching about this, but it's not the only matter at the center of my theology, nor was it the only thing at the center of Jesus's own theology.)

> You can live in the reign of God today. You can cast off the stultifying, self-aggrandizing, ungenerous ways that the world encourages us to live and, instead, show compassion, mercy, justice, and love.

So, in the end, what Jesus called people to and calls people to today is not behavior calculated to merit some eternal prize. Rather, Jesus calls us to great, radical love without judgment. We are urged, in other words, to see Christ himself in every other person, from homeless women to pompous Wall Street wizards to helpless babies. I think the Unity School of Christianity misses a lot of what traditional Christianity teaches, but I do like Unity's emphasis on recognizing the Christ in me and, in turn, having that Christ greet and welcome the Christ in you.[14]

In recent decades some scholars have engaged in the silly sport of arguing that Jesus of Nazareth never existed. It takes a wild stretch of scholarly irresponsibility to wind up with that conclusion. Heck, even Bart D. Ehrman, the University of North Carolina scholar who enjoys challenging Christianity in countless ways, acknowledges that Jesus really lived about the time the New Testament says he did.[15]

But if it could be proved that Jesus himself was a fictional character, it would strip Christianity bare and lead to unemployment for scholars such as Ehrman (who is no longer a believer). Would the ideas of compassion, mercy, justice, and radical love without judgment still have value? Yes, but people who now identify as Christian would be unplugged from any meaningful, ultimate source and rationale beyond expediency and mere survival. And the old question of whether we can be good without God would inevitably turn up this response: Yes, but why should we be?

Traditional Christianity not only insists that Jesus lived on Earth some two thousand years ago, it also insists that Jesus is alive today and active in the world. As Christian Wiman has written, we may believe God is distant but "it is false comfort, for it asks nothing immediate of us.... To believe in—to serve—Christ, on the other hand, is quite difficult, and precisely because of how near he is to us at all times."[16] Christ is in the person sitting next to you on the bus, in the autistic child next door, in the letter carrier who drops things off for you every day, in your spouse, in your children, in the politician who, by your calculus, gets everything wrong.

Faith is recognizing—and behaving as if—each of us is a child of God and that we are all Christopher, the name of my special-needs forty-something stepson whose name means "Christ bearer." Would that everyone in the world would bear Christ in the simple, beautiful, joyful way that our Christopher does. Then others, like Chris, could live today in what Jesus called the kingdom of heaven and quit worrying about whether they'll merit heaven after death. Chris knows that, as he says, "Jesus is in your heart," and he

> Jesus calls us to great, radical love without judgment.

knows that his several special-needs friends who have died now live "in heaven," as he says. But mostly he just wants a hug and wants to give you a hug so that you will know you are loved in this hour of this day. Authentic faith wants you to hug and be hugged in that way, too, though, in the end, it's more complicated than that. But not for Christopher. And perhaps we all should learn from him.

LET'S TALK ABOUT THIS

Does the idea of heaven—either for the afterlife or the kingdom of heaven Jesus spoke about being available in this life—make any difference in your life? If so, how?

What would "radical love without judgment" look like? Are you capable of it?

Can we survive an encounter with God?

One reason faith is necessary and maybe even unavoidable is that we are incapable of encountering or comprehending the divine in any exhaustive way. We long for such an experience, of course. So much so that, as Psalm 42:1–2 puts it, "As the deer longs for streams of water, so I long for you, O God. I thirst for God, the living God. When can I go and stand before him?" (NLT).

Be careful what you wish for. We may wish for a convincing appearance of God's presence, and Christian mystics report having experienced something like that. But, of course, some of the mystics in many religious traditions have been dismissed as insane, as people who've forgotten to take their meds. Still, what wouldn't each of us give to have a personal visit from the ruler of the cosmos to explain the mysteries of theodicy, to tell us how to put a square peg in a round hole, to reveal for sure who shot JFK and whether it was a conspiracy, to diagram one of William Faulkner's longest sentences, to tell us that our dead grandparents are living happily ever after? And on and on.

This irresistible desire for—and, frankly, fear of—confronting the living God leads us to the silliness of anthropomorphism, in which we create God in our image, some avuncular drinking buddy with all the answers. It's also what attracts us to Jesus, especially his fully human nature, because, truth be told, that's the best we're going to get this side of paradise in response to our desire for a personal encounter with God.

We can, of course, choose to wander around the world expressing disappointment that God doesn't respond to our feeling that we're entitled, as a child of God, to an audience. Or we can face what seems to be the harshness of God's absence and silence with a realization that God is speaking to us—or trying to—every day. God speaks to us through what early Protestant reformer John Calvin called the "theater of God's glory," nature.[17] God speaks not just through scripture, but also through the wind, the rain, the sunset, and the whole environment, which is one more reason humanity must be a conscientious steward of planet Earth (a task at which we've failed pretty spectacularly, especially since the start of the Industrial Revolution). God, after all, is every bit the artist that novelist Stanley Elkin declared him to be in his delicious and slightly sacrilegious fictional book, *The Living End*.[18] Although, of course, Elkin's artist God discovered that human beings never, ever understood that it was all about the art, so (spoiler alert) in disgust God wipes the canvas clean.

> To see God in nature, in art, in beauty of any kind, including the beauty of other human beings, requires a mature faith.

To see God in nature, in art, in beauty of any kind, including the beauty of other human beings, requires a mature faith that is satisfied, for now, with something less than a personal appearance by God. If we can accept such indirect insights about God we won't be left panting for (or making up) some special, personal visitation of the glorious presence of the Lord, which in the Hebrew Scriptures is called the *Shekhinah* (in the English transliteration). It's what turned the face of Moses to an astonishing brightness after an encounter with that divine presence. The *Shekhinah* is what dwelt in the tabernacle of the people of Israel as they wandered in the desert. I am not suggesting that God can't or doesn't do self-revelation now and again in some form that we might recognize as the *Shekhinah*. But if you think you have experienced that, you might want to check with others around you to make sure the meal you just consumed wasn't tainted with poison.[19]

Faith says, simply, that just a little taste of God probably is even more than I can handle, but let me try. Faith is satisfied to sense God's presence in the soft words a pastor sets loose on the breeze at a grave-side service, not needing a booming voice from heaven to declare at that moment that the deceased "is my child in whom I am well pleased." If you were to hear such a voice of divine intervention it might just kill you. Indeed, author Annie Dillard writes:

> I do not find Christians, outside of the catacombs, suf-
> ficiently sensible of conditions. Does anyone have the
> foggiest idea what sort of power we so blithely invoke
> [when we ask for God's presence]? ... The churches are
> children playing on the floor with their chemistry sets,
> mixing up a batch of TNT to kill a Sunday morning. It
> is madness to wear ladies' straw hats and velvet hats to
> church; we should all be wearing crash helmets. Ush-
> ers should issue life preservers and signal flares; they
> should lash us to our pews.[20]

Rather than demanding that God show up in person in all her power and might, faith simply seeks a tender assurance that someone besides us ultimately is in charge, responsible, willing to make eternal decisions in our best interest. It trusts that there really is such a someone, because to imagine otherwise would leave us forever abandoned, our lives meaningless in a world devoid of purpose.

Walk softly, God. Leave the big stick at home.

But please don't yell at us, God. Don't burst into our rooms at night and kick us awake with lightning bolts and declarations of final judgments. Walk softly, God. Leave the big stick at home. Make us not your frightened objects but, instead, instruments of your peace, channels of your grace. That will be enough. And if it's not enough, then please temper our hunger for you just enough to let us survive until it is enough.

LET'S TALK ABOUT THIS

What's the closest you've come to having a personal experience of God's presence?

If other people ever described to you a personal experience of God, did you believe them or did you just think they were nuts? What made you think that?

What is mysticism's role in faith?

A s I've at least hinted, I do not consider myself a mystic or connected in any meaningful way to the Christian mystical tradition.
Yet I recognize that the sunrise story with which I began this book
pointed to an experience that clearly had a mystical quality to it.

I also realize that from time to time others have pointed to their
own similar experience and have declared that it has mysticism written
all over it. I'll give you an example.

Some years ago I began, almost inadvertently, to act in a certain
way when taking Holy Communion in the traditional Presbyterian
family-style way, in which tiny cups and pieces of bread on trays are
passed from one person to the next in the pews. When the cup arrived,
I would hold it between the first fingers and thumbs of both my hands
so that my digits formed a sort of stylized infinity sign with the cup of
liquid in the center.

As I held Christ's blood in this symbolic infinity's center, I also
noticed that my own pulse was giving the movement of life to what
was about to give renewed life to me. The surface of the liquid would
move as the rhythmic pulsing of my blood set up a response in the
blood of Christ.

One day in casual conversation with a friend at church I explained
what I was experiencing in Communion. His reaction: "I didn't know
you were a mystic." Until then, it hadn't occurred to me that this experience had anything to do with mysticism. But I think my friend was
right. We Presbyterians, after all, believe in the "Real Presence" of

Christ in the sacrament of Holy Communion (even if most Presbyterians don't know it, and even if we don't give a name to how that happens as our Catholic friends do by calling it transubstantiation). So what I was sensing as I watched Christ's blood thump-thump to the rhythm of my own blood was the reality of the divine presence. And what else is mysticism except a personal experience of the presence of God?

So maybe once in a while I'm a mystic, following a path found in many faith traditions. In Islam it's Sufism; in Judaism, the way of Kabbalah. In every tradition mysticism moves its followers toward the presence of the very God they crave but also fear. In Catholicism, for instance, it would be hard to put together any reasonably representative list of saints that didn't include some well-recognized mystics.

> As I held Christ's blood in this symbolic infinity's center, I also noticed that my own pulse was giving the movement of life to what was about to give renewed life to me.

What I think distinguishes Christianity from some other faiths, especially so-called Eastern religions, is that as mysticism moves us toward the presence of God, the ultimate goal is not to become consumed and absorbed by that God (though, of course, we also affirm that in some mysterious way we live *in* God). One way to think about it is to say that in some Eastern traditions, the individual, represented as a drop of water, eventually falls into the sea of the divine and is forever after unrecognizable as an individual. Rather, he or she has become part of the God-ocean.

In Christianity (and the other Abrahamic faiths of Judaism and Islam), we are drawn toward God but, in the end—even after death—we in some way mysteriously retain our individual identity. There is a core essence of who we are that, by God's grace, remains autonomous and in relationship with God (or, for those who believe there's a real hell, out of relationship with that God).

Thus, you hear Christians at funerals saying that Uncle John now has joined his previously deceased wife, Aunt Rhoda, and they are enjoying a heavenly reunion. That is a concept of individuality (maybe drawn too much from America's idea of the rugged individual) that, as a rule, you won't find articulated in Eastern faith traditions. And by "Eastern" I don't mean the Eastern Orthodox branch of Christianity but, rather, traditions such as Shintoism, Hinduism, Confucianism, Taoism, and so on—or even Buddhism, which is a nontheistic spiritual path, meaning it does not postulate the existence of a god.

> In every tradition mysticism moves its followers toward the presence of the very God they crave but also fear.

In Christian terms, then, faith is a trust in the continued wholeness and individuality of each person, though, as I've already noted, not a belief in the soul's immortality. Rather, what God intends to redeem is not just a disembodied soul. Neither is that disembodied soul what God intends to absorb into God's own self until it is unrecognizable. God intends instead to redeem the whole person and, beyond that, the whole creation. The experience of that, you can bet, will be mystical, to say nothing of mysterious. And, well, a hoot. ("Hoot" is the technical theological term for joy, as in: "Let the fields and their crops burst out with joy! Let the trees of the forest sing for joy...." [Psalm 96:11–12 NLT]).

LET'S TALK ABOUT THIS

What's the closest you've ever come to having a mystical experience of God? Did you talk about it afterward with anyone?

What do you picture when you think about God redeeming the whole of creation?

Is there a place for art in faith?

A long both sides of the sanctuary of the church I call home you will find fabulous stained-glass windows. And looming over the back of the sanctuary is a Tiffany triptych stained-glass window depicting the parable of the Good Samaritan.

Our pastor, the Reverend Dr. Paul T. Rock, did a sermon series once highlighting all those windows.[21] He called it "Stained and Broken," and, of course, the windows were metaphors for the stained and broken people in the pews who, given the right circumstances, also could shine forth in whole and wholesome beauty. (There. I just reduced his whole sermon series to less than a sentence.)

From the very beginning, from what we can tell, religious faith has ushered in all kinds of creativity, including magnificent works of art. Naturally, this has led to debate. In Christian history you will find people arguing over whether any kind of art is appropriate for display in worship settings. The great iconoclastic debates of the eighth century come to mind—a struggle between people who used icons as metaphor, myth, and allegory, and those who wanted much more literal depictions or none at all. (Sound familiar?) You will find some people who think we should take one of the Ten Commandments literally when it says that we should not make any graven images. Early in the Protestant Reformation, for instance, some reformers cleared the sanctuaries of all art— to say nothing of musical instruments. And, of course, we know that the matter of art is a hot topic in such faiths as Islam, in which depicting the Prophet Muhammad is forbidden in an attempt to prevent idolatry.

What inspires religious art is a faithful desire to express the inexpressible, to give sound to silence, to incarnate and praise the invisible, the holy. So the motivation for sculpture, paintings, music, liturgical dance, some architecture, and other forms of art is pure and good, mostly. Such creativity suggests that we know our limitations when it comes to capturing the essence of the divine. So we must come at it by indirection, by representations that symbolize but do not duplicate what we're seeking to lift up as sacred.

I have no artistic skills, which is to say that, except for the ability to write an occasional clear sentence and the amateurish ability to carry a tune when I sing, I am no artist. Had I stuck with (or relearned) the oboe, which I played in junior high school and high school, things might have been different. But I gave in to the idea that my oldest sister, Karin, a Juilliard School of Music pipe organ graduate, would have to carry the family load when it came to artistic endeavors. And she has, fabulously. (While my sister Barbara, a great nurse, has been a wonderful photographer and my sister Mary has been not just a church choir singer but also a creator of unique products for teachers. Artists all.)

Still, I am drawn to religious art, and oftentimes that's what I focus on when I visit places such as the Nelson-Atkins Museum of Art in Kansas City. The more traditional (and old) the art is, the better for me. My ability to draw much meaning out of modern, more abstract art is limited, and for that I fault myself, not the artists—though surely here and there among such modern artists are people who are happy to be pulling the wool over our eyes in exchange for recognition and financial reward.

But I have come to think that beautiful religious art is not a waste of resources. One day a few summers ago I was in Washington, D.C., for the annual conference of the National Society of Newspaper Columnists. When the conference ended, my wife and I and a couple of friends went to the Washington National Cathedral to attend the 4 p.m. Sunday evensong service there in the choir lofts at the front of the sanctuary.

The choir was practicing when we arrived, singing Psalm 145, which begins, "I will exalt you, O God my King, and bless your Name for ever and ever" (NIV).

The lovely voices rose to fill the incredible space that is the main part of the cathedral.

Just before the start of the service, the ropes keeping us out of the choir lofts came down and we were invited to find a place in the lofts. I had been to the cathedral before. I'd even been to an evensong service years ago, when I also sat in the choir lofts. But on previous visits, I hadn't wandered around in the building from the observation deck to the lower levels. Oh, my. There are chapels and artistic treasures everywhere.

Yes, it's a house of worship but also an art gallery and museum, all in one.

Yet a structure like this raises a profound question: Why spend so much money on a beautiful building (not only in its initial construction but in years and years of additions and restorations) when so many people are hungry and homeless and in all kinds of economic need?

I used to think that such extravagant expenditures were wasteful. But, as I say, I've pretty much changed my mind. I think of a building like the National Cathedral as a work of art. And art is its own excuse for being. Among other things, art inspires humanity to reach beyond itself. Is there a better definition of ministry than that?

Faith finds inspiration in the arts, especially in music. I've even written a few hymns (just the lyrics, not the music) myself and I find it thrilling when someone responds by telling me how much those words meant. There is a place for just the words—poetry. And there is a place for just the music. But when the poetry combines with the music to form a new creation, faith snaps to attention, faith feels that its hammering heart, with John Wesley's, is strangely warmed.

It might well be possible to live a life of faith without the assistance of art. But it would be a shabby, drab kind of faith that could not lift its eyes unto the hills, from whence its help comes. It would be a colorless faith in a world that wants to offer us bright and gaudy gifts. It would be a silent, morose faith that does not know why the caged bird warbles.

If I had the skills, I would set this chapter to music and sing it to you. What would you do if I sang out of key? Would you stand up and walk out on me? I can't create music, so I get by with a little help from my friends. And because of that my faith sings lustily for the creative arts.

LET'S TALK ABOUT THIS

If you were part of a congregation given $100,000 to spend either on art for the sanctuary or on feeding hungry people, how would you vote? Why?

What kind of art best speaks to your sense of the sacred—painting, sculpture, music, dance, writing, or something else? Why?

How are we to respond to evil?

In several places in this book so far I have touched on the question of evil and suffering, which I now will face more directly. Theologians call this the issue of theodicy, or why there is evil in the world if God is all-good and all-powerful. It is the open wound of religion. All theodicies ultimately fail and we are left without an exhaustive answer that will satisfy us.

This is not, of course, anything like a new question. No doubt it got raised when Cain killed Abel and broke Adam and Eve's (metaphorical) hearts. But as Martin Luther King Jr. once said to a grandfather whose grandson was killed in the civil rights movement, no words can fix what happened but please know that God was the first to shed tears over this death.

Some people can be brutal in their assessment of God because of the existence of illness, suffering, evil, and death. In early 2015, for instance, British comedian Stephen Fry did a television interview in which he described God as "utterly evil, capricious, and monstrous."[22] And he wasn't done yet: "Why," he asked, "should I respect a capricious, mean-minded, stupid God who creates a world which is so full of injustice and pain? Because the God who created this universe, if it was created by God, is quite clearly a maniac, utter maniac. Totally selfish. We have to spend our life on our knees thanking him?! What kind of god would do that?"

I like the man's passion, but his understanding of God seems to have been radically, if not intentionally, uninformed by Christian theology.

What Christianity postulates is not a puppeteer god who easily could cure cancer, keep bullets from killing children, and provide health and healing on demand (which is what the "Prosperity Gospel" preachers suggest God does). Rather, God in the Christian vision is the one who comes to us in weakness, walks with us, suffers with us, cries with us, loves us through the dark valleys, and promises in the end to put everything to rights by redeeming all of creation. There clearly is a monarchial, all-powerful view of God in Christianity that in some ways is helpful in understanding God's radical otherness, but, thanks to the incarnation, what is much more to the point when it comes to our daily lives is that we have a God who holds our hand and soaks up our grief within God's own infinite heart, which now has the human nature of Jesus also at its center.

This is a difficult concept for many people. Many of us assume that an omniscient and omnipresent God could and should fix the world so as to prevent evil. (See Stephen Fry.) But that is not at all a Christian notion—and certainly not in light of the cross. We must rid ourselves of the idea that God is the source of suffering and, instead, understand God as the source of comfort in a world where love of God is possible only because we have free will to reject that very God—the free will that D. H. Lawrence once described as "my dark forest, my freedom."[23] Human participation in and complicity with evil may burden God, break God's heart, but it does not ultimately defeat God or God's vision for a final redemption of creation.

I am typing this soon after news outlets are full of descriptions of how ISIS terrorists in the Middle East caged and burned alive a captive Jordanian pilot—just days after beheading two Japanese captives. This kind of malignant evil suggests that humanity is so corrupt as to be irredeemable. Given the long history of malicious behavior by the human species, from early tribal conflicts to the pinnacle of evil, the Holocaust, and beyond, such a conclusion seems reasonable. But Christianity insists that God will have the final word. Indeed, God already has spoken that word at the empty tomb of Jesus Christ on Easter morning. Death is a goner, though it's still flailing and kicking, often in demonic ways.

Faith calls us to testify to this reality, to act as if we believe it's true. Which means that faith calls us to be present with those who suffer, to be channels of God's grace. The Reverend Jerry K. Robbins, formerly a Lutheran campus pastor, writes:

> Those who stand with victims in the name of God witness to the truth that God's love can reach into the most desperate situations and redeem them. Such extraordinary empathy declares that things are not always what they seem. While it appears that evil has triumphed, the reality is that love is stronger than evil. The abiding truth that sounds over the battlegrounds of life is that God's love is from everlasting to everlasting. It remains and abides to conquer the evil that has called it forth. It is this love that repairs the wounded heart and restores balance to the mind plagued by the problem of evil.[24]

While we stand in amazed silence at all the evil and suffering in the world and then seek ways to respond, let's also remember that faith challenges us with a question I raised earlier, which is how we explain all the goodness in the world, all the mercy, compassion, love.

I suspect God is tired of us spending endless hours arguing about the nature of evil and trying out yet more theodicies when we should be at work trying to alleviate suffering and, as God's representatives, standing with those who are wounded. The wounded are all around us, waiting for us to mediate God's healing and presence to them. So before reading on here, you have my permission to go do that. Now.

LET'S TALK ABOUT THIS

What's the best answer you've come up with for why there is suffering and evil in the world? Does having that answer help? How?

How much of the evil and suffering in the world do you believe is caused by religion itself?

Why do we need ritual?

Something in our souls, our psyches, our spirits craves ritual. It surprises me to discover that I can write such a sentence after spending much of the first half of my life thinking of ritual as often-empty actions signifying precious little, just rote, meaningless activities that people do to comfort themselves when they have no idea what else to do. No doubt there were and still are some rituals that fall into that category.

But now I am drawn to ancient customs, old practices, pregnant rituals that point to some deep significance beyond themselves. The Protestant sacraments of baptism and of Holy Communion certainly fit that description. Those and other rituals—funerals, wedding ceremonies, bar and bat mitzvahs—are ways that we touch something of the realities toward which our metaphors, our allegories, and our myths point.

Faith, in fact, might dry up and wither away without ritual, might suffocate under the weight of a limitless ad-hocness that, in the absence of ritual, no doubt would loosely guide religious life. Faith requires the kind of freedom that only discipline and boundaries can provide, and discipline is the freight that ritual carries.

But there are cautions about ritual that should not be ignored. As the Reverend Susan Marie Smith writes, "rites can be death dealing.... One thinks of the rituals of the Third Reich in Germany." And "rites can be meaningless, referring to nothing." This sometimes means that people just go through the motions, she writes, "and never open themselves to the Spirit of God."[25]

So using long-established ritual requires discernment about how it may speak to those who will participate in it and those who will simply watch it, for if ritual damages relationships and shuts down hearts, it is worse than useless. But properly and wisely employed, it can inspire us, put us in touch not only with the divine but also with our own truest selves.

Until I met the woman (then an Episcopalian) I married in 1996, I had never participated in the Anglican (and Catholic) close-of-the-day service called Compline. That was evidence that my worship experience was too limited. But it turns out that Compline has been around for damn near ever. At least it has roots as far back as the sixth century and the monk Benedict. Imagine that people have been saying these same words for fifteen hundred years or so.

From that ritual, Marcia and I have drawn a brief prayer that we say together each night at bedtime: "Guide us waking, O Lord, and guard us sleeping; that awake we may watch with Christ, and asleep we may rest in peace." (And, yes, of course we make sure we include the semicolon.) It's a ritual that comforts us, giving us a sense of continuity not just within our relationship but also with the rest of the Christian world and Christian history.

Can ritual lose its power, its sting, its ability to move our hearts? Of course. Sometimes it does. But just as often it's our fault and not the fault of the ritual itself. Sometimes it's just a case of immaturity and misunderstanding.

For example, years ago good friends at my church brought their older (but still quite young) son to worship on a day when Communion was served—a monthly occurrence in our tradition. The next Sunday Phillip's little brother Michael also wanted to come to worship. So his parents brought him, too, and he sat still, on his best behavior, the whole hour. When it ended, he broke into tears.

"What's wrong, honey?" his mother asked him. Between sobs, Michael answered, "Phillip told me we'd get snacks."

Snacks. That's all Communion meant to the little boys at that age. It would take years before they grasped the centrality and meaning of the ritual and began to integrate it into their lives. Sometimes, of course, that never happens and the meaning of the ritual passes by, unabsorbed by those in attendance. As I write this, I'm just back from a trip to the San Francisco Bay Area, where I attended a Hindu wedding. Beforehand, the priest did his best to explain in English what would be happening, but much of the ritual was said, or chanted, in Sanskrit. So although I understood that the bride and groom were joining their lives in wedlock, the sounds coming from the priest were a bit like gibberish to me. I didn't want them to be. I wanted to dive into the core of the ritual, but the language barrier kept me out, and yet not completely.

Ritual nurtures faith, helping it to stand up to the inevitable buffeting that life brings—the shocks, the disappointments, the wounds, and even to what we sometimes think of as the undeserved joys. Ritual gives faith context. And without context we are simply lost, unmoored, untethered to any core worthy of our attention and respect.

LET'S TALK ABOUT THIS

What rituals—sacred or secular—have meant the most to you? Why?

What rituals have lost their meaning for you and have become something you hope you never have to be part of again? What turned you off about them?

What can creeds teach us?

When I served in the 1980s on a committee that had oversight of some Presbyterians preparing to enter ordained ministry, each year the candidates were required to write a new statement of faith. These were sort of personal creeds that summarized the essential tenets of Christianity as each candidate understood them. It was a useful exercise not just for the candidates but also for those of us trying to get a sense of whether those candidates were growing in their grasp of the meaning of faith and ministry.

The experience of serving on the Heartland Presbytery's Committee on Preparation for Ministry led me to think anew about the eleven statements of faith, or confessions, contained in *The Book of Confessions*, which makes up the first of the two parts of the constitution of the Presbyterian Church (USA).[26] These often-detailed confessions begin with the Nicene Creed and include the Apostles' Creed, the Scots Confession, the Heidelberg Catechism, the Second Helvetic Confession, the Westminster Confession of Faith, the Shorter Catechism, the Larger Catechism, the Theological Declaration of Barmen, the Confession of 1967, and what's called A Brief Statement of Faith, which is a 1983 document created when the United Presbyterian Church in the United States of America joined the Presbyterian Church in the United States to form the Presbyterian Church (USA). The Belhar Confession, with roots in South Africa, has been approved to be the next one added to the collection.

Ranging over almost two thousand years of church history, these confessions were sincere efforts by various generations to describe what they believed and how they intended to live their lives in light of those beliefs. They're all wonderful and they're all failures. They're wonderful because they reflect the reality that throughout Christian history, followers of Jesus have taken their faith seriously enough to want to describe it in words. They're all failures because, in the end, words cannot capture the entirety (or maybe even the essence) of faith. In that sense, this book is also a failure—unless it succeeds in convincing you that words cannot capture faith in all its aspects.

But despite the inadequacy of words to describe healthy faith, I applaud those who did their best to write confessions for their era that reflected the conditions and issues of their time. Perhaps my favorite creed in *The Book of Confessions* is the Theological Declaration of Barmen, written in the Nazi era as a way to say to Adolf Hitler and his thugs that those who wrote the creed refused to think of Hitler as somehow more important than Jesus. As the declaration says, "We reject the false doctrine, as though there were areas of our life in which we would not belong to Jesus Christ, but to other lords...."

Some Christian traditions—think primarily of Baptists—describe themselves as noncreedal. Many Baptists may agree that some creeds have value, but traditionally they've been unwilling to create authoritative language that binds adherents to particular ways of expressing beliefs because they are aware that, later, they may feel a need to use different words in such statements of faith. In some ways I understand the reluctance to put faith into words. As soon as you do, as I say, you have failed and, what's worse, you've given others an opportunity to argue with you about what you got right and what you screwed up. But every written confession of faith offers a new opportunity to think theologically, to reimagine (or reconnect with) God, to find new metaphors, allegories, and myths to shine light on the divine. If constructive faith does nothing else, it should help people think theologically. At every turn in daily life, the minds of people of faith should be filtering reality through the lens of theology, the lens of faith. As a Christian, I should be asking whether I am seeing Christ in the liquor store clerk who just sold me a six-pack of beer. We Christians should be wondering whether the politician we just read about who is electing to stand against equality under the law for LGBTQ people when it comes to marriage is driven by a sincere but misguided theology or is simply a bigot in most aspects of her or his life.[27] We should be looking at the fall of autumn leaves and the accelerating expansion of the cosmos and asking about how the creation came to be and whether there's a benevolent creator or whether, instead, everything happens just by random chance. We should be paying attention to the dying and wondering where they're going. We should be listening to the groans and cries from victims of violence and hatred and wondering about what role God plays in suffering. We should be mindful, as the Buddhists say, about what is around us, and in our mindfulness should discern the presence of the spirit of the living Christ.

That's what written creeds can help us do—as long as we remember that they can never exhaustively define the parameters of faith and as long as we simultaneously pay attention to the many common threads of belief that have run through the church's most revered confessions from the beginning. If we find ourselves rejecting the long and consistent witness of scripture and of the confessions, which are always a secondary authority after scripture, we would do well to wrestle with our disbelief within a community of faith—not to prevent us from heresy but, rather, to learn how the church universal has held to these core tenets for two thousand years while we have decided that the church is wrong. It may be a humbling journey. And if the church and its members can use anything today, it's some humility.

LET'S TALK ABOUT THIS

Do you have a favorite formal confession (or statement) of faith? What especially appeals to you about it?

Have you ever written a personal statement of faith? If you wrote one twenty years ago, how might it differ from one you'd write today?

Why is the cross so central?

A small Navajo metal cross hangs on a silver chain that is almost always around my neck when I'm awake. It combines the Catholic and Protestant traditions about the cross. The Catholic crucifix traditionally displays Christ's body on the cross, symbolizing Jesus's death on our behalf. The Protestant cross traditionally is empty, signifying the importance of the resurrection. I think both traditions are right, so my Navajo cross, purchased years ago in New Mexico, shows what appears to be an empty cross, but closer examination reveals that it is textured to suggest the presence of a body, and the ends are flared to suggest hands and feet.

I wear this cross to remind my absentminded soul that this symbol is at the center of Christianity. Yes, had Jesus been executed in the United States within the last forty or so years, his followers might well be wearing small electric chairs around their necks. But the cruel wooden cross was the tool of capital punishment in Roman-ruled Jerusalem two thousand years ago, and it has become a sign of redemption and hope.

Any talk of the cross, however, inevitably leads to questions about what's called the "atonement," which is to say theories about how what happened to Jesus on the cross and what he did there resulted in that facile term we throw around, "salvation," for us. One truth about theories of the atonement is that almost everyone has one. And, like theodicies, eventually they all fail. Or, as theologian Donald G. Bloesch writes in *Essentials of Evangelical Theology* (volume 1), "No theory in and of itself exhausts the truth in the mystery of the atonement."[28]

How many theories of the atonement are there? Oh, make up a large number and you're probably close to right. Also, it depends on how you count and name them.[29]

So we must approach ideas about the atonement carefully and humbly, while never taking our wondering eyes off the cross, the meaning of which is impossible to exhaust. Yet if it's true that all atonement theories finally fail, the truth is that some fail more spectacularly than others. In his book *Healing the Gospel: A Radical Vision for Grace, Justice, and the Cross*, artist, theologian, and blogger for *Sojourners* magazine Derek Flood makes the persuasive argument that what's often called the penal substitutionary theory of atonement—which has many followers and has had since soon after Saint Anselm of Canterbury proposed its immediate predecessor in the eleventh century—is misguided and biblically out of touch.[30] Beyond that, he argues, this theory misses the message of the gospels, which is one of grace, reconciliation, and restorative—not retributive—justice. Emerging church movement guru Tony Jones makes a similarly persuasive case against the substitutionary atonement theory in his book *Did God Kill Jesus?* "God," Jones concludes, "definitely did not require the blood sacrifice of an innocent victim in order to atone for human sins."[31]

The problem is that if you get a theory of the atonement horribly wrong, you miss much of the point of the whole Christian religion. Which is to say that by sticking with the penal substitutionary theory of atonement, Flood argues, people who struggle with feelings of shame and worthlessness often assume that their image of an angry, condemning God is correct and, in fact, biblical. But, he says, that's not what the New Testament teaches at all. What the Bible teaches, he argues, is not punitive justice but restorative justice. Jesus's whole ministry, he says, was a demonstration of restorative justice. And, of course, he's right.

So what does this mean for commonly heard atonement theories and Christian theology generally? It means that Christians should set aside the strict construct that Jesus had to die to appease the wrath of a God who was angry about our sins. That image grows out of the penal substitutionary theory of atonement. A more biblical theory would describe the crucifixion as the ultimate act of love on God's own part, an act that demonstrates to us how much God loves us and an act that ultimately restores us to a right relationship with God.

In effect, adopting this more biblical approach does away with the need to scare people by telling them they're condemned to hell unless they claim Jesus as their personal lord and savior. That's punitive justice, if it's justice at all. It gets it backward. It's not that God loves us because Christ died, it's that Christ died for us because God loves us. Restorative justice seeks to create a loving relationship between us and God. In Christian theology, it allows us to see the world through the eyes of Christ. Pope Francis puts it this way: "Faith does not merely gaze at Jesus, but sees things as Jesus himself sees them, with his own eyes: it is a participation in his way of seeing."[32] So not only is Christ in us, as Christians often say, but in a strange and wonderful way, we also are in Christ.

> It's not that God loves us because Christ died, it's that Christ died for us because God loves us.

This relationship cannot, of course, simply wipe away the ways in which we have hurt others, ourselves, God, and the planet. "Mending," writes British author Francis Spufford, "is not the same thing as never broken." He continues:

> We are not being promised that it will be as if the bad stuff never happened. It's amnesty that's being offered, not amnesia; hope, not pretense. The story of your life will still be the story of your life, permanently. It will still have the kinks and twists and corners you gave it. The consequences of your actions, for you and for others, will roll inexorably on. God can't take these away, or your life would not be your life, you would not be you, the world would not be the world. He can only take from us—take over for us—the guilt and the fear, so that we can start again, in hope. So that we are freed to try again and fail again, better.[33]

The full-empty, Protestant-Catholic, Navajo-universal cross that brushes my chest all day long thus reminds me that God has loved me enough to die for me and to free me to try again and fail again, better. What I am called to do in response is to live a life that expresses gratitude for that inexpressible gift. Pretty simple, really. Except, of course, I fail at that every day, as does everyone else, which is why we needed the cross and forgiveness in the first place.

LET'S TALK ABOUT THIS

Do you think people should wear the cross, an instrument of death, as jewelry? If so, what makes that all right? If not, why not?

Do you have a theory about the atoning work of Christ that helps you understand it? If so, what is it? Or is this one of those mysteries you're willing to let professional theologians worry about?

What, finally, is the goal of faith in our time?

There are dozens of religions in the world and almost that many ways of counting them.[34] Humanity has no shortage of choices when it comes to faith traditions.

The final matter I want to take up related to faith and doubt (more fully than I already have) is whether it ever might be possible for adherents of those many religions to live in harmony and to respect one another, despite their theological differences. A candid accounting of history doesn't give us much hope, but that doesn't mean it's not worth trying to turn the ocean liner of religious history around.

Much of my journalism and faith work has been focused on interfaith relations and the need for better understanding and respect between and among adherents of different religions. Indeed, as I've mentioned, my last book, coauthored with my pastor, had to do with improving Catholic-Protestant relations.[35] I am far from alone in promoting interfaith understanding as a good idea. From the Pluralism Project at Harvard University[36] to the Greater Kansas City Interfaith Council[37] (and similar councils around the country), many people have dedicated themselves to educating others about faith traditions different from their own and to gaining the experience of personally knowing people who pledge allegiance to those traditions. Many people, yes, but not enough.

Although the demographics are changing, the United States remains a country in which the vast majority of citizens identify themselves as being some variety of Christian, even if just a so-called nominal one.[38] Increasingly, however, such Christian citizens are working with and living near many adherents of non-Christian religions. In parts of the country you will find certain enclaves densely populated with members of non-Christian faiths, such as the many Hindus in the south San Francisco Bay Area and the many Muslims in and around Detroit. Another example: Los Angeles has a significant Buddhist presence. And, of course, the Pacific Northwest is known as the land of the "nones," those religiously unaffiliated people who, when asked to identify their religious affiliation on a list of faiths, choose "none of the above."

This growing diversity calls for a thoughtful response, but it cannot be simply a Kumbaya, syncretistic effort that assumes it will be easy to get along and that all religions are pretty much the same. That's the road to trouble. If, however, we can hold to our own faith traditions firmly and yet be respectful of the choices others make, we have a chance.

That's why I've been so insistent in this book that we approach faith with humility, recognizing that we are limited in what we can know with certainty and how much of the divine we can comprehend. False certitude leads not just to arrogance but also to imagining that everyone else is wrong about faith and that it's up to us to straighten out a misguided world. Can we be what Rabbi Brad Hirschfield, whom I mentioned earlier, calls both deep and wide when it comes to faith? Can you personally invest hours and hours trying to grasp what theologians mean when they talk about soteriology or eschatology and then acknowledge that your understanding is not the final one, that others in different traditions may have valid insights that you don't? And, more to the point, that you may be wrong about what you think you know?

That's the combination of a commitment to a faith path and a commitment to humility and openness that is required if America is to be a model for how a religiously diverse population can live together in peace and respect. It is no easy task. But there must be leaders who can set the tone, can move others toward this same commitment by calling into question their persistent condemnation of whatever religion is not theirs. This struggle for openness, humility, and wisdom cannot be won with the tools that radio and TV talk show hosts currently employ—scoring rhetorical points by outshouting others and ignoring or distorting facts. Rather, it must proceed with civil discourse, with a firm gentleness that breaks down barriers and brings new eyes to see what we could not see before.[39]

Faith can fuel this effort. Faith, grasped at least partly through doubt, can give us the stamina to endure a broken world in which people imagine that faith is either all or nothing. Faith can keep us focused on the goal of demonstrating what a world of peace, harmony, mercy, justice, and love might look like. Faith can show us the substance of things hoped for, the evidence of things not seen until that longed-for day when, at last, sight replaces faith and we all walk in the light that is the light of the world. This is the very light that came into the world and emblazoned the darkness, a darkness that could not extinguish it so that, in the end, we will see the glory of that light, which is full of grace and truth and that dwells among us. May it be so.

LET'S TALK ABOUT THIS

If you were asked to describe the beliefs and traditions of a religion other than your own, which one would you be most comfortable picking? Why?

How many "nones," those who claim no allegiance to any religion, do you know? What do you most admire about their choice and what do you think they're getting wrong?

Abbreviations

In references to passage of scripture quoted in the text of this book, these abbreviations are used for various translations of the original Hebrew and Greek into English:

CEB   Common English Bible

KJV   King James Version

NIV   New International Version

NLT   New Living Translation

NSRV   New Revised Standard Version

Notes

Introduction

1. Throughout this book, when I quote scripture, I will use several different translations—and sometimes they may be versions with which readers are not familiar. A list of abbreviations appears on page 138. One reason is that I collect different translations of the Bible because I find it helpful to compare how the original Hebrew and Greek (and a bit of Aramaic) is rendered into English by various translators.

Approaching Doubt

1. The books to read on this topic are Robert W. Jenson, *Systematic Theology: The Triune God*, vol. 1 (New York: Oxford University Press, 1997) and Miroslav Volf, *Allah: A Christian Response* (New York: HarperOne, 2011), especially the chapter titled "The One God and Holy Trinity."

2. As 1 Corinthians 3:19 has it: "For the wisdom of this world is foolishness in God's sight" (NIV).

3. Christian Wiman, *My Bright Abyss: Meditation of a Modern Believer* (New York: Farrar, Straus and Giroux, 2013), 72.

4. Kurt Vonnegut, *Palm Sunday* (New York: Delacorte Press, 1981), 330.

5. I am not going to give you a link or reference to the *Left Behind* books. You can look up that silliness for yourself.

6. The red stew story, found in Genesis 25:27–34, is about Esau and Jacob, sons of Isaac and Rebekah. Esau is an outdoorsman, Jacob a home boy. Esau comes in from the field one day hungry, as Jacob is cooking a stew. Jacob convinces Esau to sell him his birthright in exchange for the stew, a short-term fix that makes Jacob, who later is called Israel, the heir apparent.

7. N. T. Wright, *Simply Good News: Why the Gospel Is News and What Makes It Good* (New York: HarperOne, 2015).

8. Frost spoke at a September 2011 conference I attended in suburban Kansas City presented by the Sentralized Missional Church Conference.

9. The book to read is Barbara R. Rossing, *The Rapture Exposed: The Message of Hope in the Book of Revelation* (New York: Basic Books, 2005).

10. Wright, *Simply Good News*, 16.

11. For much more on Paul and his Jewish context, see the work of, among others, religious scholar Mark D. Nanos, which you can access at http://marknanos.com. Also see the book of which Nanos is the coeditor, *Paul within Judaism: Restoring the First-Century Context to the Apostle* (Minneapolis: Fortress Press, 2015).

12. Wright, *Simply Good News*, 16–17.

13. Ibid., 132–33.

14. The book to read is Dietrich Bonhoeffer, *The Cost of Discipleship* (New York: Touchstone, 1995).

15. Bill Tammeus, *A Gift of Meaning* (Columbia: University of Missouri Press, 2001), 152–53.

16. Karl Barth, *The Epistle to the Romans* (New York: Oxford University Press, 1968).

17. Richard Rohr, *Falling Upward: A Spirituality for the Two Halves of Life* (San Francisco: Jossey-Bass, 2011), 54–55.

18. Marilynne Robinson, *The Givenness of Things* (New York: Farrar, Straus and Giroux, 2015), 103.

19. For the full poem, see Ezra Pound, "Hugh Selwyn Mauberley," Poetry Foundation, http://www.poetryfoundation.org/poem/174181 (accessed May 13, 2016).

20. Brian McLaren, *A Generous Orthodoxy: Why I Am a Missional, Evangelical, Post/Protestant, Liberal/Conservative, Mystic/Poetic, Biblical, Charismatic/Contemplative, Fundamentalist/Calvinist, Anabaptist/Anglican, Methodist, Catholic, Green, Incarnational, Depressed-yet-Hopeful, Emergent, Unfinished Christian* (Grand Rapids, MI: Zondervan, 2004).

21. Jacqueline A. Bussie, *Outlaw Christian: Finding Authentic Faith by Breaking the "Rules"* (Nashville: Nelson Books, 2016), 46.

22. Ibid., 39.

23. Burton Z. Cooper, "Why, God? A Tale of Two Sufferers," *Theology Today* 42, no. 4 (January 1986): 433.

24. Dallas Willard, *The Allure of Gentleness: Defending the Faith in the Manner of Jesus* (New York: HarperOne, 2015), 27.

25. To read the whole remarkable poem, see "The Love Song of J. Alfred Prufrock," http://www.bartleby.com/198/1.html (accessed May 9, 2016).

26. One of Brad Hirschfield's best books is *You Don't Have to Be Wrong for Me to Be Right* (New York: Harmony Books, 2007). You can read about him and the book at his website, http://www.bradhirschfield.com/author.html (accessed May 9, 2016).

27. John Calvin, *Institutes of the Christian Religion*, vol. 1, translated by Henry Beveridge (Grand Rapids, MI: William B. Eerdmans, 1989), 128.

28. Makoto Fujimura, *Silence and Beauty: Hidden Faith Born of Suffering* (Downers Grove, IL: IVP Books, 2016), 49.

29. One good place to keep track of that landscape is "The American Values Atlas," *Public Religion Research Institute*, accessed May 9, 2016, http://ava.publicreligion.org/home#religious.

Taking Doubt Seriously

1. See my book, *Woodstock: A Story of Middle Americans* (Bloomington, IN: AuthorHouse, 2014).

2. The book to read is Thomas G. Long, *Accompany Them with Singing: The Christian Funeral* (Louisville: Westminster John Knox Press, 2009).

3. Shirley G. Guthrie Jr., *Christian Doctrine* (Louisville: John Knox Press, 1968), 381–82.

4. For more on that and other atonement theories, see my later chapter "Why is the cross so central?"

5. Kenda Creasy Dean, *Almost Christian: What the Faith of Our Teenagers Is Telling the American Church* (New York: Oxford University Press, 2010).

6. In 2012, Finn was convicted of the misdemeanor of failing to report to government authorities suspected child abuse by a priest in his diocese. Eventually, in April 2015, Finn resigned under pressure.

7. Bill Tammeus and Jacques Cukierkorn, *They Were Just People: Stories of Rescue in Poland During the Holocaust* (Columbia: University of Missouri Press, 2009).

8. The book to read is *The Cloud of Unknowing*, translated by Evelyn Underhill (Digireads.com, 2011).

9. The story of the misplaced blessing is told in Genesis 27.

10. Tammeus, *Woodstock*, 44.

11. Caitlin Doughty, *Smoke Gets in Your Eyes: And Other Lessons from the Crematory* (New York: W. W. Norton, 2014), 214.

12. The book to read is Atul Gawande, *Being Mortal: Medicine and What Matters in the End* (New York: Metropolitan Books, 2014).

13. Bill Tammeus, *A Gift of Meaning* (Columbia: University of Missouri Press, 2001).

14. To read about the care Kansas City Hospice & Palliative Care provides, see Eric Adler, "A Good Death: As End of Life Nears, an Unexpected Friendship Forms in KC Hospice," *Kansas City Star*, April 23, 2016, www.kansascity.com/news/local/article73547107.html.

15. See "America's Changing Religious Landscape," *Pew Research Center*, accessed May 12, 2015, http://www.pewforum.org/2015/05/12/americas-changing-religious-landscape. A more detailed collection of statistics about this can be found in "The American Values Atlas," Public Religion Research Institute, accessed May 11, 2016, http://ava.publicreligion.org/home#religious.

16. The book to read is Kelly Brown Douglas, *Stand Your Ground: Black Bodies and the Justice of God* (Ossining, NY: Orbis Books, 2015).

17. Jürgen Moltmann, *The Crucified God: The Cross of Christ as the Foundation and Criticism of Christian Theology* (New York: HarperCollins, 1974), 201.

18. Julie Galambush, *The Reluctant Parting: How Did the Followers of Jesus Stop Being Jewish?* (New York: HarperSanFrancisco, 2005).

19. Annie Dillard, *The Writing Life* (New York: Harper & Row, 1989), 3.

20. For more on Newell, see *Heartbeat: A Journey Toward Earth's Wellbeing*, accessed May 9, 2016, http://heartbeatjourney.org/j-p-newell.

21. John Philip Newell, *Listening for the Heartbeat of God: A Celtic Spirituality* (Mahwah, NJ: Paulist Press, 1997), 10–11.

22. Ibid., 38.

23. Ibid., 2.

24. To read the whole creed, see "Athanasian Creed," accessed May 9, 2016, https://www.ccel.org/creeds/athanasian.creed.html.

25. See my previous remarks about theologian Paul Tillich in the earlier chapter "What can we learn from the Celts?"

26. Annie Dillard, *Pilgrim at Tinker Creek* (New York: Harper & Row, 1974), 137.

27. The full text of this speech can be found at "Remarks by the President at National Prayer Breakfast," *The White House*, accessed May 8, 2016, https://www.whitehouse.gov/the-press-office/2015/02/05/remarks-president-national-prayer-breakfast.

28. Jay Michaelson, "Breaking Down President Obama's Point about Christian Crusades and Islamic Extremism," *Huffington Post*, last modified April 9, 2015, http://www.huffingtonpost.com/jay-michaelson/obama-crusades-islam-_b_6635750.html.

29. Ibid.

30. Ibid.

31. "Santorum: President Obama Needs a History Lesson," *Iowa Republican,* last modified February 5, 2015, http://theiowarepublican.com/2015/santorum-president-obama-needs-a-history-lesson.

32. A book to read to understand the roots and depth of the racism that has marked American Christianity is by Kelly Brown Douglas, *Stand Your Ground.*

Faith in Light of Doubt

1. Kurt Vonnegut, *Palm Sunday* (New York: Delacorte Press, 1981), 78.

2. One book to read is Adam Hamilton, *Seeing Gray in a World of Black and White: Thoughts on Religion, Morality, and Politics* (Nashville: Abingdon Press, 2012).

3. See Frank Newport, "In U.S., 46% Hold Creationist View of Human Origins," *Gallup,* June 1, 2012, www.gallup.com/poll/155003/Hold-Creationist-View-Human-Origins.aspx.

4. See "Haida," the Kids' Site of Canadian Settlement, Library and Archives Canada, accessed May 11, 2016, https://www.collections-canada.gc.ca/settlement/kids/021013-2061.2-e.html.

5. W. Somerset Maugham, *Of Human Bondage* (New York: Doubleday & Company, 1936), 486.

6. Quoted in "The Opinions of Anatole France," *The Nation* 114, no. 2966 (May 10, 1922): 566.

7. Walter Isaacson, *Benjamin Franklin: An American Life* (New York: Simon & Schuster Paperbacks, 2003), 88.

8. Mother Teresa and Brian Kolodiejchuk, *Mother Teresa: Come Be My Light: The Private Writings of the Saint of Calcutta* (New York: Image, 2009).

9. Jacques Ellus, *Hope in Time of Abandonment* (New York: Seabury Press, 1973), 173.

10. Ibid., 176.

11. Christian Wiman, *My Bright Abyss: Meditation of a Modern Believer* (New York: Farrar, Straus and Giroux, 2013), 166.

12. Ellus, *Hope in Time of Abandonment,* 177.

13. Ibid., 178.

14. If you don't know about Unity, which was founded and still has its international headquarters in the Kansas City area, you can learn about it at *Unity,* accessed May 11, 2016, http://www.unity.org.

15. The book to read is Bart D. Ehrman, *Did Jesus Exist?: The Historical Argument for Jesus of Nazareth* (New York: HarperOne, 2013).

16. Wiman, *My Bright Abyss,* 120.

17. For a good discussion of this idea from Calvin by Dr. Belden C. Lane, professor of theological studies at St. Louis University, see "John Calvin on the World as a Theater of God's Glory," *Oxford Scholarship Online,* http://bit.ly/1CyN4GG, doi:10.1093/acprof: oso/9780199755080.003.0004.

18. Stanley Elkin, *The Living End* (London: Jonathan Cape, 1980).

19. To explore the idea that God is not just within existence but is existence itself, see Doug Pagitt, *Flipped: The Provocative Truth That Changes Everything We Know about God* (New York: Convergent Books, 2015).

20. Annie Dillard, *Teaching a Stone to Talk* (New York: Perennial Library, Harper & Row, 1982), 40.

21. Paul is coauthor with me of *Jesus, Pope Francis, and a Protestant Walk into a Bar: Lessons for the Christian Church* (Louisville: Westminster John Knox Press, 2015).

22. For more details, see Henry McDonald, "Stephen Fry Calls God an 'Evil, Capricious, Monstrous Maniac," *The Guardian,* February 1, 2015, http://bit.ly/16i1b4D.

23. D.H. Lawrence, *"Benjamin Franklin," Studies in Classic American Literature* (New York: Viking, 1923); the quote is found online at http://xroads. virginia.edu/~HYPER/LAWRENCE/dhlch02.htm under "13. Humility."

24. Jerry K. Robbins, "A Pastoral Approach to Evil," *Theology Today* 44, no. 4 (January 1988): 493.

25. Susan Marie Smith, *Caring Liturgies: The Pastoral Power of Christian Ritual* (Minneapolis: Fortress Press, 2012), 3.

26. You can find a free downloadable version of *The Book of Confessions* at The Office of the General Assembly, accessed May 9, 2016, https:// www.pcusa.org/resource/book-of-confessions.

27. For my essay on what the Bible really says about homosexuality, see "The Bible and Homosexuality," *Bill's "Faith Matters" Blog,* accessed May 8, 2016, http://bit.ly/q0T102.

28. Donald G. Bloesch, *Essentials of Evangelical Theology,* vol. 1 (New York: Harper & Row, 1982), 152.

29. Two books that will give you good lists of atonement theories are Daniel L. Migliore, "The Person and Work of Christ," in *Faith Seeking Understanding: An Introduction to Christian Theology* (Grand Rapids, MI: William B. Eerdmans, 1991), and Shirley C. Guthrie Jr., "Is God Against Us? The Doctrine of the Atonement," in *Christian Doctrine* (Atlanta: John Knox Press, 1968).

30. Derek Flood, *Healing the Gospel: A Radical Vision for Grace, Justice, and the Cross* (Eugene, OR: Wipf & Stock, 2012).

31. Tony Jones, *Did God Kill Jesus?: Searching for Love in History's Most Famous Execution* (New York: HarperOne, 2015), 235.

32. Pope Francis, *Walking with Jesus* (Chicago: Loyola Press, 2015), 3.

33. Francis Spufford, *Unapologetic: Why, Despite Everything, Christianity Can Still Make Surprising Emotional Sense* (New York: HarperOne, 2013), 164.

34. At *ReligionFacts*, for instance, the list includes more than seventy names of faith traditions, though in addition to Christianity the list, oddly, includes many Christian denominations as if they were separate religions. See http://www.religionfacts.com/religions (accessed May 13, 2016).

35. Rock and Tammeus, *Jesus, Pope Francis, and a Protestant Walk into a Bar.*

36. See *The Pluralism Project*, accessed May 9, 2016, http://pluralism.org.

37. See the Greater Kansas City Interfaith Council, accessed May 8, 2016, http://www.kcinterfaith.org.

38. That majority, however, is becoming less vast. A 2015 report from the Pew Research Center showed that between 2007 and 2014, the percentage of Americans identifying as Christian dropped from 78.4 to 70.6. The full report is at "America's Changing Religious Landscape," Pew Research Center, May 12, 2015, http://www.pewforum.org/2015/05/12/americas-changing-religious-landscape/.

39. The books to read are Os Guinness, *The Case for Civility: And Why Our Future Depends on It* (New York: HarperOne, 2008); James Calvin Davis, *In Defense of Civility: How Religion Can Unite America on Seven Moral Issues That Divide Us* (Louisville: Westminster John Knox Press, 2010); and Richard J. Mouw, *Uncommon Decency: Christian Civility in an Uncivil World*, 2nd ed. (Downers Grove, IL: IVP Books, 2010).

Suggestions for Further Reading

Bussie, Jacqueline A. *Outlaw Christian: Finding Authentic Faith by Breaking the "Rules."* Nashville: Nelson Books, 2016.

Flood, Derek. *Healing the Gospel: A Radical Vision for Grace, Justice, and the Cross.* Eugene, OR: Wipf & Stock, 2012.

Hamilton, Adam. *Seeing Gray in a World of Black and White: Thoughts on Religion, Morality, and Politics.* Nashville: Abingdon Press, 2012.

———. *Making Sense of the Bible: Rediscovering the Power of Scripture Today.* New York: HarperOne, 2014.

Hecht, Jennifer Michael. *Doubt: A History: The Great Doubters and Their Legacy of Innovation from Socrates and Jesus to Thomas Jefferson and Emily Dickinson.* New York: HarperOne, 2004.

Newell, John Philip. *The Rebirthing of God: Christianity's Struggle for New Beginnings.* Woodstock, VT: SkyLight Paths Publishing, 2014.

Plunkett, Stephen W. *This We Believe: Eight Truths Presbyterians Affirm.* Louisville: Geneva Press, 2002.

Robinson, Marilynne. *The Givenness of Things: Essays.* New York: Farrar, Straus and Giroux, 2015.

Spufford, Francis. *Unapologetic: Why, Despite Everything, Christianity Can Still Make Surprising Emotional Sense.* New York: HarperOne, 2014.

Wiman, Christian. *My Bright Abyss: Meditation of a Modern Believer.* New York: Farrar, Straus and Giroux, 2014.

Printed in the USA
CPSIA information can be obtained
at www.ICGtesting.com
JSHW082211140824
68134JS00014B/561